# THORNY PATH TO FREEDOM

## The Story of the No-Tax Campaign in Uttara Kannada 1932-33

Dr. Suryanath U. Kamath

Popular Prakashan
www.popularprakashan.com

Published by
POPULAR PRAKASHAN PVT. LTD.
301, Mahalaxmi Chambers
22, Bhulabhai Desai Road
Mumbai – 400 026



First Published 2010



(4378)

ISBN 978-81-7991-630-8

Design & Typesetting: Sunita Rane

Printed in India
by Repro India Limited
Mumbai

Published by
Ramdas Bhatkal for
Popular Prakashan Pvt. Ltd.
301, Mahalaxmi Chambers
22, Bhulabhai Desai Road
Mumbai – 400 026

# FOREWORD

"Truth is stranger than fiction" it is said. Dr. Suryanath Kamath the veteran historian has narrated the happenings during Salt Satyagraha, No-Tax Campaign and Jungle Satyagraha with minute details that are the hallmarks of genuine fiction.

That Gandhiji's call could reach even the poorest in remote corners of Karnataka, inspire them to face bullets, lathis and ill-treatment by the British police seems to be almost unbelievable. Call it history or fiction or by any other name this is the truth witnessed by the historian Dr. Kamath.

He has done enormous groundwork, collected facts from hundreds of participants in the struggle for freedom and met every one of the characters in the novel. His family participated in the freedom struggle when he was a boy.

But what is amazing is Dr. Kamath's sense of the novel form. He creates a host of characters, their characteristic way of speech, their emotional world, their way of life and Gandhiji's influence on their lives. They become haunting symbols in our minds. Reading the novel becomes an experience. The novel is like a piece of architecture carved out of the huge rock of experience.

Sumatheendra Nadig
(Former Chairman, National Book Trust)

## ABOUT THE AUTHOR

Dr. Suryanath Upendra Kamath, M.A., Ph.D. is a scholar of history, renowned researcher and creative writer in Kannada. Born at Beltangady, D.K. Dist. in 1937, he secured his M.A. degree in 1959 from Karnataka University and Ph.D. in history in 1965 from Mumbai University. He had a stint as a journalist, working in *Free Press Journal*, Mumbai and later in *Utthana* (Kannada monthly) and *Prajavani* (Kannada daily).

He was a Lecturer and Reader in Bangalore University (1968-81) and was Chief Editor, *Karnataka Gazetteer*, Govt. of Karnataka (1981-95) and held concurrent charge as Director of Karnataka State Archives (1981-83). He has edited *Karnataka State Gazetteer* in two volumes and its Kannada version in three volumes. Seven District Gazetteers are also edited by him. As a historian, his book in Kannada on Karnataka History won him State Sahitya Academy 1st Prize for humanities in 1973 and his monograph on John Fleet (noted historian) secured him Bangalore University research award in 1980. The Karnataka government conferred Rajyotsava Award on him in 1999 for historical research.

His *Swatantrya Sangramada Smritigalu*, a three volume publication in Kannada of 3,200 pages contains reminiscences of 850 freedom fighters. He is also the author of *Quit India Movement in Karnataka*. He was the President of Mythic Society and now the President of Karnataka Ithihasa Academy. He was a Member of Indian Council of Social Science Research (Delhi) and was Chairman of Raja Rammohan Roy Library Foundation, Kolkata (2000-2003). He is editing *Quarterly Journal of the Mythic Society* from 1977.

He has penned four novels in Kannada. One on the Vijayanagara Emperor Krishnadevaraya has been translated into Hindi. The present work in English is the rendering of his novel *Mullina Hadi* based on the freedom movement.

# PREFACE

The late Sri Shankar Gulwadi, renowned freedom fighter and Sarvodaya worker from Uttara Kannada ( N. Canara District) is the inspiration behind this venture of mine, the Kannada novel *Mullina Hadi* (Thorny Path). It was first published in 1976 and has gone into several editions. I have myself translated the novel into English. However, Sri Gulwadi's earnest wish to make it as a film was not fulfilled. Five episodes based on accounts from the book were serialised on television in Kannada, and five more in Hindi.

The No-Tax Campaign in the course of the Civil Disobedience movement was launched in Bardoli taluk of Gujarat, and it had great leaders like Sardar Patel. It got much publicity and was also prominently mentioned in the volumes on the freedom movement. But the one launched in Canara (Karwar District) though more severe, with participants being more firm, persevering and undergoing greater suffering, did not get due recognition and publicity.

Sri Gulwadi, who was a student in Wilson College in Mumbai, gave up his studies, came to Canara with a batch of similar young men in 1920. He lived in Canara, participated in all the important campaigns of the freedom movement (1920-21; 1930-34 and 1942), served long jail terms and continued as a Sarvodaya Worker. He remained a bachelor calling himself "Sarvakara Sevaka", to serve all in the socicty, and especially those families who had suffered in the freedom movement. He passed away in 1983.

Sri Gulwadi and I sat together while scripting the work in Kannada. I had interviewed nearly 100 persons who had participated in the No-Tax campaign in Canara in my three volumes in Kannada (running into a total of more than 3,200 pages), *Swatantrya Samgramada Smritigalu*, which also contains first-person accounts from 850 freedom fighters from Karnataka. The volumes were published between 1974 and 1980 from Mysore by Gita Book House. I was a lecturer in history in the Bangalore University then.

Except Krishnaswamy and Rukmini who are imaginary characters, almost all characters in this novel are real (names changed in some cases) and all episodes are factual. This gives us an idea of how their innocent patriotism was unsung and unwept. They fought with determination against the British in a non-violent fashion. It is an epic struggle of sacrifice. I must plead my incapacity to depict all episodes more effectively and thus I am presenting only some glimpses of the whole movement. I am happy that Sri Shankar Gulwadi enjoyed my presentation.

My former colleague in the Bangalore University, noted Kannada poet and writer and former chairman of National Book Trust, Dr. Sumatheendra Nadig has corrected the script and offered his valuable comments. It has been further edited by Sri Gokarna of Popular Prakashan. Sri Sadanand Bhatkal and Sri Satyajit Bhatkal have taken the risk of publishing it. My sincere thanks to all of them.

Suryanath U. Kamath
198, XI Main, Suttanna Kanagal St.,
Hanumantanagar, Bangalore 560019

# CONTENTS

# The Hideout

"They stopped him at Kalkani, outside the village and gave him a shave."

"Shave? Why a shave?" asked Gulvadimam.

"Shaving the head and beard was a minor expiation. He was administered *panchagavya.*"

All present laughed loudly.

"Gulvadimam, it did not end there – there were fire rituals and he was made to change his sacred thread. That was the major expiation."

"That also was done?" asked Gulvadimam.

"Not only that. They said, 'You had gone to jail. In the jail, no one knows who supplies water and who cooks the food, who knows what was their caste? You fool, by having been to jail, you have brought bad reputation to our family. Go to Goa, go to Partagali Math and have yourselves stamped with hot *mudra.*' So saying they sent him to Goa."

There was loud laughter again.

"Consenting to go to Goa, he went straight to Sirsi, offered Jungle Satyagraha there, and is now imprisoned at Hindalgi Jail. This is the attitude of our Puranik."

"In what way is Shinna Kamat related to Puranik?" Gulvadimam asked.

"He is the younger brother of Puranik. But he was given in adoption to Kamat family; so he is called Shinna Kamat. Now it is said that they have issued a warrant to arrest this Puranik. That is the news…."

"How do you know this?"

"You know our 'wireless system'. But my worry is, will Puranik pay land tax, or will he go to jail?"

"What will he do, Mahabala?" asked Gulvadimam.

"There are many who have not paid land tax. They have signed the pledge also that they would not pay. But Puranik never showed any great enthusiasm about Civil Disobedience."

"Has he signed the pledge that he would not pay?"

"Yes, he has. But he does not have much land. The land he has is a small piece. He gets a rent of two bags of rice. His dues are only fourteen annas, anyway not more than one rupee. It looks like Puranik's wife told the Ugrani that they will not pay. Second time when Ugrani came, Puranik was not there. Now they have issued a warrant," said Mahabala.

"Look Ganapa, we must meet Puranik now," Gulvadimam said.

"What is the use? 'Why have you come here? You want to send me to jail?' he may angrily question us. He may also abuse us."

"No, he will not abuse me," said Gulvadimam.

"Sure he will not abuse Gulvadimam," Ganapa Bhatt said.

"Look Mahabala you accompany Gulvadimam. I won't come. But Gulvadimam, do you know, old women in our Havik Brahmin community especially the widows, have great faith in Puranik. He gives consecrated ash and they administer it as medicine to young children if they have any minor ailments. Don't you know this Mahabala?" Ganapa Bhatt said.

"Yes, yes that is a speciality. People from all the villages around Bonagiri, Bedkani, on this side, Itagi, Kyadgi, people from all these villages come to him and he gives consecrated ash for fever, infection or other such problems. They place one *duddu* and pray. He asks them to pray and to apply ash to the forehead of the patient and also make the patient partake a small quantity of the ash. People feel their children are cured," Mahabala told Gulvadimam.

"Is it a fact? This is really nice. In case Puranik is arrested, we shall organise a protest march of these old women," said Gulvadimam.

"You mean a procession of the widows?" Ganapa Bhatt asked.

"Why not?" said Gulvadimam.

"Your idea is excellent. But will Puranik be ready to get arrested? It is this very Puranik who had subjected his brother, two months back, to various expiations for having been to jail. Will he himself now go to jail?" Ganapa Bhatt raised his doubt.

"He had signed the pledge, is it not? Let us talk to him. Are you joining us, Krishnaswamy? Do you still feel tired?"

"No, I had a sound sleep in the afternoon. I'll join you," Krishnaswamy said.

"Who is this new young man?" Ganapa asked.

"This is Krishnaswamy. He has come from Bangalore. Yesterday he had reached Sirsi and today he is here. He belongs to Sevadal. Today Mhala Pai left him here. He will work with us. Last time, in 1930 he was at Ranebennur, and he had been imprisoned for six months for offering Satyagraha there. He was in Hindalgi jail. Now Advocate Sampige Vekatapatayya from Bangalore has deputed him. He reached Goa by boat and reached Gokarna. Jois has sent him here. We must assign work to him," Gulvadimam explained.

"That is really nice. Your name is Krishnaswamy, isn't it? Dear sir, a lot of work is here. But if you speak your Mysore style Kannada, you will be caught and sent straight to Hindalgi jail. You must pick up the local strain of Kannada soon." When Ganapa Bhatt said this all started laughing loudly. Krishnaswamy too had a hearty laugh.

"I am trying to pick up the local slang," said Krishnaswamy. Ganapa Bhatta imitated Bangalore style Kannada and Dharwad style with all its subtle laughable points. All laughed aloud.

"Haaa, Hooo," a loud voice was heard, piercing the darkness of the night.

"Somebody appears to be approaching us. See Mabala, who is that," Gulvadimam said.

The boy who made the loud noise from a distance, came running. He was an observer from a distant treetop, keeping an eye on the visitors—whether they were friends or foes. If they were policemen, he signalled, "Hooo..Haaa." If friends, "Haaa Hooo." The boy announced: "Pundlik Shenoy and some other person are coming."

"If it is Pundlik Shenoy then he knows the path." Ganapa took a lantern and went out. Soon Ganapa returned, and loudly announced, "Gulvadimam, it is Puranik that is coming."

Gulvadimam was surprised. "Give me the lantern. If it is Puranik, I must receive him," and went out with others.

"Salutations Puranikji, I am Gulvadi Shankar. You have taken the trouble of visiting our hideout!" Gulvadimam said. Puranik returned salutations. Straightaway he entered the hut.

"I have been forced to come and see you. I was told that they have issued warrant to arrest me. So I heard…."

"I also heard the news. It is nice….," Gulvadimam said.

"You feel it is nice?" said Puranik.

"For non-payment of land tax, nobody has been arrested in Bilgi town. In case they begin with you, they will have started an arresting spree with a worthy person. It augurs well. Who can be a better person than you to help us to start our work?"

"It is not that…I am not afraid of going to jail."

"Is that so!" Gulvadimam exclaimed, with the mixed feeling of pleasure and surprise.

"Not only I am not afraid of going to jail, but also I am not afraid of facing a gunshot. Look here, my youngest child is nine months old. And my wife is carrying and about to deliver in the next two months. In the rainy season, in the lunar month of Jyestha, she is sure to deliver. My brother Shinna has gone to jail. His adopted mother who stays with us is suffering from bronchitis. There is nobody at home. The youngest child is not keeping good health. In addition to that, in the lunar month of Vaishakha, my daughter's marriage is scheduled. It can't be held in the rainy season, you see? My wife's delivery is due…. With all these problems, how to manage these affairs, you please tell me Gulvadi," Puranik poured out his problems.

"What advice can I, of all the persons give you? What is it that you are not aware of? In this *dharma yuddha* who all have to lay down their lives, I can't say," said Gulvadimam.

"Yes Gulvadi, I know it fully well. What all has to be offered in this sacrifice, has to be offered. I am not afraid of death. I have signed the pledge. Shinna's mother has also signed the pledge paper. What is bound to happen will happen. I will not pay revenue even if I am reduced to cinders."

Though surprised, Gulvadimam told Puranik, "I was sure that you will take such a firm stand."

"But if I am taken to jail, what will be the shape of things to come? Shouldn't I consider all that? What happens to my household? Suppose they confiscate our household goods. I have not got our thatched roof redone. In the rainy season it starts dripping…," said Puranik.

"What I think is this. You have tied the *kankana,* lifted the *veelya.* When the battle will start is the question. They have selected you as the first to be arrested. They want to create terror in the minds of the townsmen, that is my impression. When will they serve the warrant?"

"It looks they have instructed Jamadar Jamal to arrest me first. When he was being instructed, Sirsi Imam's brother-in-law, Karim overheard it. He told me," said Puranik.

"Karim doesn't lie. We had news from Siddapur station too over the matter."

"Right then Gulvadi, the information is correct. Now what shall I do?" Puranik asked.

"This ploy to threaten you and also the townsmen with action to be taken against No-Tax payers, is a trick. Please tell everybody that they have issued warrant against you. Your bedding is ready and you are preparing to enter jail. It may have its own effect. You had got expiatory rites performed for your Shinna Kamat's going to jail might have created an impression in the minds of the people that you will shudder to think of courting imprisonment. They might be expecting that you will tender an apology and pay the tax. If one person pays the tax, others will follow suit. This may be their calculation. That is why, it looks to me they have made you the first target," Gulvadimam said.

"What! I apologise? Look here Gulvadi, I swear with my sacred thread in my hand that I will not apologise. I am a Brahmin. When I signed the pledge, everything was decided. I came to share my problems with you, that is all," Puranik said.

"I know your firmness. You are a Vedamurthy. You are one who has studied the Vedas, Puranas. You are an enlightened person. The uneducated people of the Namadhari caste, Kannanayak and Kariyanayak from Bedkani, the Nadavars and the Halakki caste men did not pay tax last year and their properties were confiscated by the government. Already they have started confiscations in our Herur region. Now at Bilgi, they want to begin with you. Yes, it is hazardous. If enlightened Vedantins like you hesitate, what will the other folk do?" Gulvadimam said.

"No, no I am not afraid. I told you the facts, the circumstances in which I am placed. I know the Sanskrit saying – if you die fighting you will attain heaven. The only problem is whether I can avoid the arrest now to cross over the hurdles I am facing. That is all," Puranik said.

Gulvadimam replied, "I have followed you fully. It appears to be a trick to terrorise people. Last year they first collected revenue from Bhagvan Shenoy. This year they have targeted you. They may keep quiet if you put up a bold face. Let us face the situation. You please be prepared to face all eventualities."

"Yes, I agree. Let anything happen. Tomorrow in the morning I shall tell everybody. Warrant is issued on me. Let us see. Now I start to go from here. It is too dark. Salutations to you all, *Namonama*."

"Let me join you till we reach the end of the road to see you off." Gulvadimam joined Puranik and his other companion.

All others entered the hut. They could not contain their laughter while they talked about the highly conservative Puranik getting ready to undertake a highly unorthodox act of going to jail.

"See Mabala, this Puranik, has strong belief about pollution. Will he go to jail?" Ganapa Bhatt asked.

"He will go. He will definitely go. Otherwise he would not have come here to meet us. Don't you know Banavasi Paramayya Bhatt went to jail last year? When he heard that his widowed sister Ganapi decided to undertake Jungle Satyagraha, he also undertook Satyagraha. Who could believe he went to jail? When he was told

'You are arrested,' his spontaneous reply to the police officer was, 'What *arishta* to me? *Arishta* (disaster) befalls your British government,'" said Ganapa, and laughed loud.

By then Gulvadimam came back, and told Ganapa, "Ganapa, early in the morning before daybreak you must reach Bilgi. I shall reach there a little later, by about seven, and wait at Pundlik's house. You all come there next. On the way you must convey the news to all the nearby villages that Puranik is going to be arrested. This message should reach all widows with red sari. They must be invited to reach Bilgi to protest against the arrest.... You Krishnaswamy, there is no need to go to Bilgi tomorrow. You change your dress, put on a three-yard *panche* in *kacche* style. Wear the sacred thread. One more *panche* to cover your torso, and wrap a long piece of cloth round your head. You must look like village Havik Brahmin Priest. You accompany Ganapa Bhatt, and go round with him for a walk. You get yourself acquainted with the area and the people. Try to pick up the local Kannada dialect......He must provide you with a local companion." Gulvadimam said again: "Let Ganapa accompany him for a day. Later we will ask Heggere Bhaira Nayaka's son Era, to be his companion. He is a very smart boy. Krishnaswamy, have you a three-yard short *panche* to wear? Your shirt will be of no use here. Your Bangalore hair cut will not work. One Krishnamurthy who came from Bangalore was apprehended only by seeing his shirt," Gulvadimam said.

"How is that?" Krishnaswamy queried.

"Having seen his neatly stitched shirt, the police realised that he was not a local person. As they were speaking to him, the police saw the label behind the collar, and identifying him as a Bangalorean, they apprehended him. Have you got a short *panche* with you? I am speaking of *panipanche* used by the priestly class. The type that we are wearing."

"I have a two-yard cross *mundu* and a four-yard *khadi panche* to be worn in *kacche* style, but not of this style."

"I shall present you one. You know how to wear it in *kacche* style?"

"Oh yes."

Gulvadimam told him: "Tomorrow morning you wear this. When you go to Bilgi buy a new pair. It costs six annas per piece. Do not trim your moustache, allow it to grow longer. Have your crop cut tomorrow in the local way and have a pig tail. Do not put on an underwear inside. The translucent *panche* exposes it. With this new garb, you will look a perfect underground worker. For the grand staging of Gandhian drama these are the costumes. You leave your slippers here and buy the local footwear which costs you one and a quarter rupee. You can also buy it at Bilgi."

"O yes?" said Krishnaswamy.

"You have cash with you?"

"For the time being *parva illa* (I will manage)."

"No *parva illa.* Don't use such words of Mysore slang. *Addi illa* is a common expression here. Do not talk to unknown persons .... till the time you pick up the local lore. Behave like a dumb person or a stammerer till that time. Otherwise you will be easily identified as an outsider and apprehended. Then your coming here will be a waste. We lose a worker," Gulvadimam said.

"I don't think there will be such a shortage. Workers, new workers will appear," said Krishnaswamy.

"Not that, this is your modesty. The intelligent workers, those who plan actions during critical situations, and those who rise to the unexpected occasions, are highly essential. Seva Dal has trained such men. Last year Matanda from Coorg, Kulkarni from Dharwad, Deshpande from Belgaum, Anantarao and Jois from Mysore, Sardar Venkatramaiah from Bangalore, Bhairappa, Vasudeva Rao and Pandit did tremendous work. Sardar Venkatramiah became famous. He was called 'Sardar', like Sardar Patel, for his planning, resourcefulness and leadership. Most of the Patels here have resigned by his efforts! Shankara, is *conji* ready? If it is, spread the leaf plates," said Gulvadimam.

"The clock has stopped at eight. I had forgotten to wind it," said Shankara.

"I have a watch. It is ten-thirty now," said Krishnaswamy.

"Oh, it is very late now. I have to get up at 4.00 in the morning."

"You Krishnaswamy, don't tie your watch on your wrist when you go out, attach it to your waist. It is good that you have your watch. Otherwise we would not have known the time. This is *vanavasa*. We are away from the civilization. If you forget to wind your watch, you will know nothing."

Shankara spread plantain leaves. Ganapa Bhatta, Mahabala Hegde, Chauda, Shankara, Gulvadimam and Krishnaswamy were the only persons present. Pundilk Shenoy and one or two others who were present in the noon had gone away. All started partaking *conji* in the lantern light. It was rice boiled with plenty of water. Krishnaswamy had partaken such *conji* only when he was sick. The corners of plantain leaf were folded in a peculiar way to make it look like a plate, so that the liquid *conji* won't overflow. Krishnaswamy also tried to do it, but he could not. The corners of the leaf got torn. Gulvadimam taught him how to do that. They served salt and poured four ladles of *conji.* The ladle was of coconut shell with a stick attached to it. Pickle made of raw mango was served in a corner of the plate. All partook *conji* and got up belching as if they had partaken *amrita* (ambrosia).

"Krishnaswamy you go to bed. Take one or two gunny sacks from that corner. They are the bedstead here. Shankara, give him a *kambli.* It is very cold here. Take this. I shall awaken you early tomorrow," said Gulvadimam.

It was a thatched hut, 20 feet long and ten feet wide. A portion of it was used as kitchen. About 100 feet away there was a stream with fresh water. But it was very shallow. With the help of a tumbler of a coconut shell one had to fill a bucket or a pitcher. Krishnaswamy had bathed there in the afternoon. In the midst of a thick jungle, clearing some trees, the hut had been built. Even from a distance of 20 feet, none realised that a hut was there. Though it was half-a-mile away from the Siddapur-Bilgi road, nobody could know its existence. The distance to reach Bilgi was just one mile. On the rugged path reaching the hut, there was a huge mango tree near it. A teenaged boy Chauda sat on a strategic point of the tree during the day and kept a watch. If any known person was seen approaching, he would shout loudly "haaaa…. hooo" to make the hut dwellers know about the visitors. If it was unknown persons or the police, the signal was "hooo….haaa". When his work in the kitchen was over, Shankara relieved Chauda. Then Chauda kept himself busy bringing water to the hut, or visiting Bilgi and attending other odd jobs or collecting firewood. Both of them were teenagers. In the afternoon two other boys of the same age had come there, and Krishnaswamy had seen them. In the night after food, Chauda had no watch-and-ward duty. In the dark night the police or other strangers couldn't reach the place. If he went out of this camp, how to return to this place was the problem Krishnaswamy faced. The forest was so thick. He had seen many anthills in the afternoon while reaching the place, and also one or two snakes. He felt chilly out of fear.

Chauda and Shankara slept at a distance from Krishnaswamy. A little further, Gulvadimam, Ganapa Bhatta and Mahabala Hegde were engaged in conversation. A lantern with its shortened wick was providing dull light.

□□

# Dreaming of Freedom

Shankara and Chauda were snoring. Krishnaswamy could not get sleep. On his discharge from Hindalgi jail, two constables had escorted him to Bangalore. In February. 1932, when the Civil Disobedience Movement restarted, he met Advocate Venkatapathiah at Bangalore and expressed his intention to join the movement. There was no movement in princely area, but only in British Presidencies. He was active in Seva Dal at Bangalore. Though ban on other front organizations of Congress had been lifted on the signing of the Gandhi-Irwin Pact, ban on Seva Dal had been continued. Dozens of youth had gone to British areas like Madras and Bombay Presidencies in 1930, and many had undergone jail terms. They had returned to Bangalore in 1931 after Gandhi-Irwin Pact. Gandhiji attended the Round-Table Conference and returned empty-handed. The movement was started again in 1932.

When Salt Satyagraha was launched in April 1930, many from Bangalore went to Ankola in North Canara. Krishnaswamy could not join them. Later he went to Hubli and Seva Dal leaders sent him to Ranebennur, the headquarters of a taluk in Dharwad district. There he joined the Jungle Satyagrahis. He was sentenced to six-months term which he spent in Hindalgi Jail near Belgaum.

But 1931 was the year when lovers of freedom were highly disturbed. The Gandhi-Irwin Pact had filled the hearts of patriotic men with confidence and courage. But government did not adhere to the terms of the Pact, and took steps to dupe the people. Everywhere in the country, and especially in the North West Frontier, the United Province and Gujarat, the freedom fighters were continuously harassed. On 12 January, Mallappa Dhanshetty and other young patriots were hanged at Sholapur. Motilal Nehru died on 6 February in the same year. Even before the tears of sorrow would dry, Bhagat Singh and other patriots were hanged on 23 March. When the whole country was in a pool of tears, Gandhiji had returned from the Round Table Conference from London empty handed to the deep disappointment of all and he was arrested soon after his return from England.

Patriotic young men like Krishnaswamy could not keep quiet. His blood was boiling. He felt like joining the movement again. He went to Hubli. The Seva Dal headquarters at Hubli had been closed. Diwakar and other leaders were in Jail. There was none to guide him. He went to Belgaum. He knew Gangadhar Rao Deshpande. He had been with him in jail. He directed him to go to Gokarna via Goa by steamer. He posed as a pilgrim, and escaped arrest on landing at Gokarna. The Police were watchful on visitors to Gokarna. The political movement was strong.

Common people supported the movement at Gokarna. Krishnaswamy had heard much about North Canara district too. He had heard much more during the last two days. This was a district with nature's bounty enhancing its beauty. On the one side there is thc roaring ocean. On the other side there are rows of green peaks of the Western Ghats. Thick green forest looked like Nature Goddess herself. In the forests were moving freely and happily animals like elephant, chital, bison, sambar, rabbit, and other wild animals. Birds like parrot, koel and other sweet singing birds were in abundance. Swinging with the wind, tall trees of betelnut, coconut, mango, jackfruit and teak abounded and loud sounding waterfalls, big and small beckoned the visitor.

In this district of natural beauty, competing with the natural forces on the one hand, and taming the nature and living in harmony with nature were the adventurous innocent people of the district.

The British considered the district as a forest region. To the government forest products and trees were more important than the people and their habitation. They were prepared to sacrifice humans for the sake of thc forests. Struggling against the nature's vagaries, leading a secluded life in thick forests, attending to agriculture, raising plantations, shedding their sweat and thus filling their belly were the hardy inhabitants. More than filling the belly, filling the State Treasury, was the main worry of the people here. People were treated like wild animals and they were afraid of government machinery.

At last the story of Gandhi's movement spread. People stood up to protest. People of all castes came alive and started breathing the idea of freedom. In towns and urban centres educated people awoke first. They were followed by the merchant class. Habib-Ullah-Khan an unknown patriot from Peshawar who had come to Dharwad for some political assemblage visited North Canara, delivered fearless speeches in all towns of the district, condemning the British and the local officials, and created an awakening among the Muslims. The Vedic Brahmins felt a sense of awakening. When leaders of freedom movement came to Gokarna, at the Mahabaleshwara temple, they used to recite the benediction in the name of the leader, "Asahayoga Siddhyartham, Swarajya Prapyartham!" The government put many restrictions on the life of the people in the name of forest laws and other regulations. Wild animals like elephants, monkeys and porcupines damaged their crops too.

In 1924 Karnataka State Political Conference was held at Gokarna and it was presided over by His Holiness the Shankaracharya of Dwarakapeeth. This created a favourable atmosphere in favour of *swaraj* in the district. People were full of enthusiasm willing to support Gandhiji's non-violent movement. The Swami condemned untouchability too.

So much was the harassment by the forest department, that they filed suits on innocent peasants and forced them to attend circuit courts. When the roads and transport facilities were poor, a peasant accused of forest offences had to visit Honnavar or Haliyal or Bhatkal or Kumta for hearing the court adjournments! If there was an incident of fire in the forest, persons in whose house there was a death were charged with damaging the forest. Even a Lingayat or a Muslim, who do not cremate the dead, were not spared! The Forest Department ran a parallel government and District Forest Officer was more powerful than the District Collector! People were weary of harassment.

The first political prisoner from the district during the non-cooperation movement (1921-22) was Bedkani Chauda Nayak of the Bedkani village. This and many other incidents, Krishnaswamy had heard at Gokarna and from other Political workers he had met in the course of two days, especially from Narayana Bhatta who had come to guide him through the hilly and forest path while coming from Gokarna to Sirsi. All these incidents Krishnaswamy remembered at night. The whole district was amidst a whirlwind of national awakening. Even the ocean looked restless!

Just a week back Gokarna temple had celebrated its car festival. During the Shivaratri Jatra, the tallest ratha (car) was pulled. Thousands of pilgrims assembled. A boy inserted a tricolour flag to look prominently among the coloured flags of the car at its top. It was done just five minutes before the car was moved. The police insisted that the tricolour flag should be removed. The volunteers who had assembled to maintain order and discipline strongly protested against the police order. People who had held the ropes to drag the car dropped the ropes and left the place. People who had assembled for the Jatra, left the place and made for the seashore. The itinerant shopkeepers covered their ware with cloth or gunny bags and walked away. Regular shops were also closed down. All these incidents occurred in no time, and the place was deserted. Nobody had asked them to do all this. Everything was spontaneous. The site of the Jatra had a deserted look. The priests who were seated near the idol on the car got down, surrounded the police officer and cursed him. "The Jatra, being held for centuries has been stopped, and you policemen will be cursed by God Mahabaleshwara, and your progeny will suffer", the priests cursed. The police officer started trembling, and left the place with all his colleagues. He saluted God with all devotion and begged for mercy. Soon people reassembled, a row of tricolour flags decorated the car and the festival was held with great pomp.

Krishnaswamy had read about the incident in an English paper. It was a four-line report. Narayana Bhatta gave him all the details. 'Is there need to prove Gandhiji's Satyagraha would win? This Gokarna incident is the best example. If the armed police could be made powerless, the British government also could be made powerless,' he thought.

When he heard the account of Salt Satyagraha of 1930 at Ankola, he was highly impressed. The Excise Department people would scratch the ground with a stick on the sea shore where a small sheet of salt would accumulate during the high tide. The sheet of salt could be used by people. The government agents did not want people to use even this freely available salt without paying the duty. If anybody was found gathering such salt, he was severely beaten with a stick by the Excise Department servants. People showed great enthusiasm over the issue of breaking salt rules. Large number of people participated in the Satyagraha in April. Congress workers had conducted a wide propaganda, visiting every house around Ankola and lecturing in every marriage pandal. Congress workers from Dharward, Haveri, Shimoga, Davangere, Sirsi, Karwar, Kumta, Gokarna came walking in procession in batches, and conducted propaganda over the proposed Satyagraha and reached Ankola.

On 13 April 1930, over 30,000 people assembled, for the Salt Satyagraha at Ankola and went in a procession from Ankola to the seashore, brought pots full of seawater, lit fire in ovens on a maidan at Ankola, waited till the water in the pot evaporated, and the 'salt' found at the base of the pot was collected and packets of salt were auctioned. Those who bought the contraband salt included rich persons like Kasala Srinivasa Setty from Davangere and Devru Nayaka, hawker of groundnut from Ankola.

"If people are to revolt on this scale, how can we rule over this land?" the District Police Superintendent and the District Excise Officer, both Europeans talked among themselves and withdrew in the evening. There was no violence and no breach of peace, though a crowd of thousands had assembled.

"Our district has observed Salt Satyagraha, Jungle Satyagraha, Hullubanni Satyagraha, No-Tax campaign on such a large scale, that if everybody joining them were to be arrested, jails in Bombay Presidency would be insufficient. On the first day of Salt Satyagraha at Ankola, the mile long procession saw every processionist shouting slogans." What Narayan Bhatt had narrated moved as real scenes in front of Krishnaswamy's eyes.

The next morning after the first Salt Satyagraha on 14 April,

M.P. Nadkarni and Swamy Vidyananada, only two were arrested. Satyagraha continued for one full month. Everyday one or two persons were arrested. The Salt Laws became ineffective. The people on their own manufactured salt for their domestic use.

Many produced salt on a large scale and organised a contraband salt market at Ankola by hoisting tricolour flag and placing Gandhiji's photo in their stalls. Hundreds of villagers bought tax-free salt to the tune of 10 to 20 seers and stocked it for their household use. All along the coast, contraband salt markets flourished. Such markets were held from Karwar to Kasarkode and Bhatkal. Government closed its eyes to this Civil Disobedience. When people untiringly protest, whom will you arrest? The high tide of protest could not be checked. It was at that time that people even attacked and looted the Hangarkatta government salt godown. The Namdhari women from the villages rose with slogans like 'Ganji Maharajku Jai', 'Ganji Sarkarku Jai'. These very village women later performed Jungle Satyagraha, and Satyagraha like non-payment of land-tax. The previous year itself there was No-Tax campaign in this district.

From Gokarna, passing through Manjuguni, Mundagesara and other places which had offered Satyagraha the previous year made Krishnaswamy feel that he was visiting holy pilgrim centres. In fact Krishnaswamy was to work in Sirsi, as per plan.

But the effort to organise No-Tax Campaign in Sirsi taluk did not get good response. Kadave Hegde directed Krishnaswamy to go to Siddapur. The Siddapur workers sent Krishnaswamy to the camp near Bilgi, after serving him breakfast.

Krishnaswamy was rapturous when he thought about the movement. He considered it as his good luck to participate in this movement in whatever capacity, as a commander or as an ordinary soldier. It was a *dharmayuddha* for him. In his sleep, Krishnaswamy dreamt that he was participating in a procession, was drafting articles for bulletins, turning the cyclostyle machine, was running in a forest while being chased by the police. In his dream he felt he was being beaten by the police and was telling his colleagues not to retaliate, and not to give up non-violence.

□□

# A Woman's Wrath

"Krishnaswamy, please get up, it is four-thirty now." When Gulvadimam said this, Krishnaswamy who was half asleep opened his eyes. His eyes were burning. "Chauda, take the lantern with him to the stream. Finish your ablutions early. We have to leave at five-thirty." Krishnaswamy with the help of the lantern light went to the stream, finished his ablutions and by the time he returned hot *kashaya* was ready. As instructed on the previous day, he wrapped himself with the handloom *panche,* covered his torso with another such piece, and head with a thin towel, and started in the company of Ganapa Bhatta. On the way they saw one or two hamlets – each hamlet had one or two houses in the middle of the areca garden.

"Ganapayya Hegde, Ganapayya Hegde…." Ganapa Bhatta called loudly. A dog started barking.

"Who is that?" a Havik housewife came out. "He is not at home," she said.

"Oh, you Ganapa Bhatru…. Wait, he has gone to the garden, I shall call him," she said and went running. The speed with which the somewhat stout lady ran surprised Krishnaswamy. "That showed her enthusiasm," he said to himself.

"Here, all males do not stay at home. Mostly women stay. Officials come for confiscation of property or to arrest; in anticipation the men hide themselves in the garden or in the fields," Ganapa Bhatta told Krishnaswamy. By then Ganapayya Hegde having wrapped himself in a country blanket, pushing snuff into his nostrils, arrived.

"Namaskara, Bhatre, come, be seated, let us have *asare* (breakfast)," he said.

"No, no *asare* now. I have to reach Bilgi via Balemane. Today they have issued the warrant against Bilgi Hanumant Puranik. They will arrest him."

"Which Puranik, *mantravadi* Puranik?" the housewife asked with curiosity and concern.

At that time, a widow with her head covered came out: "When our child had infection, he gave consecrated ashes. Is that Puranik arrested?" she asked.

"What *grahachara* is this? If they arrest him to which hell the police want to go?" she continued.

"Now all of you must reach Bilgi. If he is arrested, you must hold a protest march. Now Godakka, you go to Halasgod and also to Kelaguli on the way. Ask all women like you to attend the march. Ganapayya Hegde, you please go to Tarkhand and Paduvalli. Ramayya's mother-in-law and elder sister also may be asked to come. I will go to Balemane and then to Bilgi," said Ganapa Bhatta.

"Puranik gives consecrated ashes to all the surrounding villages. They want to catch hold of him?" widow Godakka said cursing.

"Now I am leaving Godakka. You please visit Halasgodu and Kelaguli, and reach Bilgi before eight o'clock. You, Hegde go to Tarkhanda and Paduvalli. I am going now," so saying Ganapa Bhatta left hurriedly saluting all. After walking for fifteen minutes in the forest they reached Balemane. Dogs kept on barking vociferously. There were three houses of Haviks. But all the members of the families were absent. One lady went to the garden and brought all the members from the garden. Ganapa Bhatta advised the women to go to Bilgi, explaining everything to the male members.

"It is reported that at Herur there have been confiscations," somebody told Ganapa Bhatta. "I read the news in the Bulletin."

"Yes, there have been confiscations in four houses. You all must reach Siddapur on the fourth. It is Gandhi Day. You remember what had been announced at Gunjgod?"

"Yes, we all will come," said one of them. "We all, nine of us, have decided to come." By the time Ganapa Bhatta left the place all the male members of the three households, 8 to 10 women and nearly 20 children had gathered.

"*Asare* is ready, please take it and go," said one elderly person to Ganapa Bhatta.

"No, there is no time, it is late. Kaverajji, Seethakka, all of you must come to Bilgi. Makkikatte Godakka also will come. They have gone to invite people from Halasgodu and Kelaguli. Makkikatte Ganapayya has gone to Tarkhand and Paduvalli. He will bring with him women from Paduvalli. Similarly from the other parts. People from Itagi, Haragi, Lambapura also will come. You too come. I will see you, *namaskara*," saying this Ganapa Bhatta set out. A small boy shouted, "Gandhi Sarkarku", and all who had gathered there responded "Jai". Krishnaswamy could hear the slogans till the time the hamlet vanished from his eyes. Dogs were barking loudly. Are they also joining the slogan shouters? Krishnaswamy wondered. Amidst the thick forest, toiling and raising plantations, and away from modern civilization, the enthusiasm of these farm men made Krishnaswamy highly gratified. At this rate getting freedom will not be far away, he felt.

As suggested by Ganapa Bhatta, in the next 5 to 6 days, on 4 March, there will be a big programme at Siddapur, thought Krishnaswamy. "On 4 January, Gandhiji was arrested. On 4 February, we celebrated 'Gandhi Day'. We arranged *prabhat pheri* (procession) at Siddapur. Now we are holding similar programme on 4 March. From 4 February, nobody should pay land tax was our vigorous propaganda. The first instalment has to be paid on 15 February. For the second instalment there are two more months. There are fifteen hundred land-holders in our Siddapur taluk. When we requested the *khatedars* (land owners) to sign the pledge for non-payment, the men were not in their houses. But we convinced the women at home, and persuaded 400 *khatedars* to sign the pledge. Many of these *khatedars* do not attend the weekly *shandy* at Siddapur. Except these 400 *khatedars* the rest have paid the first instalment. But *Hullubanni* (grazing tax) is not paid by hundreds. Due to confiscations, many have suffered. They have to be emboldened this year. If household items like vessels, jewellery, domestic cattle etc are confiscated, it is the women who feel distressed. Now we have conducted propaganda among women, and they are determined. Nearly seven to eight hundred people have signed the pledge, not to pay the second instalment. On 26 February, there was a meeting at Gunjgod village for the first time, and a good number of men attended. The majority of the *khatedars* in this taluk are the Havik Brahmins. Next in number are the Namdharis, that is the Divars. Our Chauda Nayaka is a Namdhari.

"In the towns of Bilgi and Siddapur there are the Konkani Brahmins. On the fourth, all of them have agreed to come. Send your women. In case you men folk do not attend, we shall organise procession by women. Men may dress themselves in saris, put on bangles and stay at home. Gandhiji has said that more than men, he has faith in our mothers. Gulvadimam spoke strongly. All have agreed to come. Now during the next six days, strong propaganda has to be undertaken," Ganapa Bhatta explained in detail.

By then, they had reached the outskirts at Bilgi.

"Now, we took a circuitous route. We came through Makkikatte and Balemane. We have walked four miles. In fact our camp is just one-and half miles from Bilgi," said Ganapa Bhatta.

"I could not follow the route... If I am asked to reach our camp from here, I have to go round and round in the forest," said Krishnaswamy.

"Don't worry. We shall provide you with a guide who will take you to all the places. There is Bilgi town. There are about 50 or 60 houses. There are also shops. A royal family of Bilgi was ruling during the Vijayanagara times, as their subordinates. Then it was a town with thousand households. With the advent of the British, the town almost shrunk. The high-handedness of the British, their policy of deforestation, the menace of wild animals, the spread of malaria, all this resulted in the decline of population. Many villages have been depopulated. The forest rules are so strict that the people are damn afraid of the forest department. The people of this district are totally anti-British because of these strict forest laws. The political awakening here started with the formation of an association called Vana Dukha Nivarana Sangha to fight forest grievances. The first meeting of the association was held at Bilgi in 1916. In this place the Konkani Brahmins are in a majority. The first district committee was organised here itself in 1921. Gulvadimam was saying so. "We are going to the house of Pundlik Shenoy. It is a huge household with 50 members. It is a house of patriots. Two persons from this house are already in jail, having offered Jungle Satyagraha."

Through a backyard path, they entered a tiled large house. "Ganapa Bhattaru has come," a boy shouted. Two women welcomed them with a smile. "Has Gulvadimam come?" one of them enquired.

"He will come in the next half an hour. Gopal Shenoy is not there?" Ganapa Bhatta enquired.

"He is there. Please get in, come to the kitchen. Breakfast is ready, wash your feet," replied the women, and then another gentleman came.

"Namaskar, Ganapa Bhatta. Who is this gentleman?" the gentleman asked. All members of the family assembled there.

"Namaskar Gopal Shenoy. This is a new worker who has come from Bangalore. We address him as Krishna Bhatta," Ganapa Bhatta said.

"Namaskar Krishna Bhatta. I am Gopal. What is this? Gulvadimam is assembling all widows. If Puranik is to be arrested, why arrange the procession of these widows? Already eight to ten have assembled near the temple. Puranik it looks, went round the town and told everybody that a warrant is issued, and he will be arrested. 'I am getting ready to go to jail,' he told everybody."

"Are they sure to arrest him?"

"Yes, they will definitely arrest him. His condition is pathetic. His wife is carrying. His daughter's marriage is fixed. What is he going to do? His announcing today that he is going to jail makes one feel that he is determined to go."

"You don't know? Last night he had come to our camp. Holding his sacred thread he swore that he would not resort to apology," Ganapa Bhatta said.

"Pundlik was telling us jokingly if men like Puranik go to jail, it means, Gandhiji's message has reached the last man and Swaraj is fast approaching. All your Havik women will go to jail. This is the man who administers sacred ashes to them you see," Gopal said.

Hot soft rice bread with *chatni* and *kashaya* were served. They talked about the spread of the movement. After the breakfast, Gopal took them upstairs, and through the window Gopal pointed out the women sitting in the premises of the temple. "Look Ganapabhatta, these women have come walking from a distance of five to six miles. I was told that some are coming from Bhuvanagiri also. Let me count.... There are 13 over there. This is an unlucky figure for the British. I shall go over there and find out who all are there," said Gopala Shenoy and he went out.

Krishnaswamy saw through the window, the widows all crestfallen. Some were young, all dressed in red sarees. As he was watching them, three more came, accompanying a boy.

"Gulvadimam's plans are *rustum*. If at eight in the morning, so many widows have assembled, by ten o'clock when Puranik is likely to be arrested, what will be the number!" Gopal wondered. "These village women, these widows, will they march in procession? Will they help us in winning swaraj?" Krishnaswamy wondered. From the moment he came to the district, he was astonished to see the type of people participating in the movement. The peculiar atmosphere here at every step caused him a strange feeling of rapture.

"Bulletin, Bulletin has come," a boy came running.

"Oh, it has come today. It had not appeared for the last four days. After the arrest of Timmappa Master, it is not appearing regularly," said Gopal and started reading it aloud. It was a cyclostyled sheet in foolscap size, handwritten.

"Is it the Bulletin?" Krishnaswamy enquired.

"Yes. For seven or eight days, some issues were reaching us in a bunch by post. Now they are issuing it from Siddapur."

"Look at the news: 'Four *japtis* (confiscations) at Herur,' '*Japti* at Dodmane,' 'The police did the confiscation even when a lady was in delivery pangs', 'Collector to visit Siddapur on Friday.' Oh

Clee Saheb is visiting Siddapur today. We must inform Gulvadimam about it."

"Gulvadimam is coming," a boy brought the news. Krishnaswamy surveyed the area. There was a huge house resembling a fort. The total area, both on the ground floor and upstairs could be five thousand square feet. There was a broad courtyard in front of the house. To the back of the house, there was a thick wild growth. In front of the house, at a distance and on the roadside, there was a huge temple. "This house is like a fort. The police, if they come from the front or from the back, one can easily escape from this house," he said to himself. Gulvadimam now came there.

"Puranik will certainly be arrested. The Sub-Inspector will come from Siddapur by the Sagar bus. Gopal, we have now to prepare ourselves. We shall take a procession of these ladies to Siddapur. What do you say Gopal?"

"It looks like Clee Saheb has come. Let him see the scene. There will be at least hundred ladies. Already there are 20 to 25. Many more will come."

"You intend to take these women to Siddapur on foot? Can they walk eight miles?" Gopal asked.

"We will ask them. Clee Saheb has camped in the circuit house. To demonstrate our fury in his presence will be an effective thing to do. We shall ask these ladies. In case some cannot walk, we shall arrange one or two bullock carts for them.... I will ask them," said Gulvadimam.

When Gulvadi approached the ladies, they agreed to walk till Siddapur. None of them wanted bullock carts. By then it was time for Sagar bus to arrive. The Police Inspector alighted form the bus. The Village Accountant, two constables and two Ugranis (village servants) also came. They straight went to Hanumant Puranik's house.

"Hanumant Puranik is present in the house?" one Ugrani asked.

"Yes, I am here. What news? You have come to collect land tax? I am not paying the tax," Puranik replied from within the house, without moving from his seat.

The Village Accountant went into the house. "See Mr.Puranik, you have to pay the land revenue of thirteen annas. Its first instalment is six and half annas. Padmavati Keshav Kamat's first instalment of land revenue is six rupees and three annas. Chautayi is one and half rupee. The total revenue now payable is rupees eight, annas thirteen and pies six. Pay this amount. Why unnecessarily create problems?"

"Dear Shanbhag, my sister has gone to Sagar. Her son has gone to jail. How can I pay their land tax?"

"Right, now the instalment of your own land revenue is six-and-half annas, grazing tax 12 annas, Chauthayi five annas. The total is one rupee, seven annas and six pies. At least pay this amount. Don't you have even this much?"

"No sir, I won't pay."

"Dear Puranik, don't say that. I will lend the amount as loan. Pay me later. Shall I write the receipt?"

"No no. Not because I do not have money. If I sell these earrings it will be more than that amount. I am not going to pay. This looting foreign government, is fit to be called a dacoit. I have taken an oath not to pay. Have you brought a warrant? You are welcome to arrest me," said Puranik standing in the centre of the front yard, lifting both his hands.

"Mr.Puranik, you are a Vydika Brahmin. You should not go to jail. This is a small amount, please pay," the Police Sub-Inspector advised him. "In case you don't pay the revenue, your house also will be seized," he continued.

"Look Saheb, I am a Brahmin. Our profession is seeking alms. I came to this world with a bare body, and will return from this world too in the same state. To this *yajna* (sacrifice), let me be the first offering."

"Where are you," Puranik addressed his wife. "Where have you gone? Look, these people mean to arrest me and seize our house. I go with them. You also don't pay them after my arrest. They will also come to seize the goods in our house. In case they do, take a burning firebrand from the oven and set the house on fire. Later we shall go on pilgrimage to Kashi and Rameshwar and earn our livelihood by seeking alms. Come on, where is the warrant? I am ready to follow you", Puranik said and he addressed his wife, "Bring my *panche* and upper garment, *uttariya*."

He was till then dressed only in a *langoti* (loin cloth). Puranik wrapped himself in his *panche,* covered his body with the upper garment and was ready to depart. The Sub-Inspector and the constables were nonplussed. Their job had been made very simple. But it was also a complicated situation. They had anticipated that Puranik might not agree to be arrested, he may resist arrest and they may have to demonstrate their 'power'. Puranik's wife and children started shedding tears.

"Do not weep, do not be afraid, God will protect us, Mahatma's truth will save us," Puranik consoled them. He stood in front of his main door near the Tulasi plant and shouted loudly: "Mahatma Gandhiku Jai."

Puranik had never participated in a *prabhat pheri,* the early morning procession. His loud slogan made the Monkey Brigade (of young volunteers) of boys and other Congress workers also join in slogan shouting. There was an assembly of nearly 400 people.

"Bolo Bharatmataki – Jai!"

"Grazing Tax – Don't Pay!"

"Land Tax – Don't Pay!"

"Vande – Mataram."

The Police party and Puranik became the vanguard of the huge procession!

The seventy to eighty widows that had assembled near the temple joined the procession. By the time they reached the Police Chauki, there was a huge gathering of people. When they came to know that Puranik will be taken to Siddapur in the afternoon by bus people dispersed. But the procession of the widows in the hot sun, proceeded to Siddapur. By the time they crossed Bilgi town their number rose to nearly 100. Near the Bhuvanagiri tank (halfway to Siddapur) all of them rested a while, partook plantains distributed to them, drank water and set out again in no time. Now their ranks had swollen to 125. By noon they reached Siddapur Circuit House and sat on its lawns.

Collector Clee was surprised to see these women in strange dress.

Early in the morning he had seen a slogan-shouting procession, consisting of nearly 200 men. By the time he could reach the Circuit House, a delegation of arecanut gardeners was waiting for him.

They represented their grievances. "Last year there was a disease which damaged our crop. Please write off our revenue dues. Now the officers are seizing and confiscating our household goods for non-payment of revenue. This is not fair. Our previous representation has not been heeded. Wild elephants, bisons, porcupines and monkeys destroy our crop. Many license holders of firearms have their arms seized and licenses cancelled under the pretext of non-payment of tax. And priests of many temples are branded as sympathetic to the Congress movement and they are not receiving annual *tasdik* or government grant to the temple. The government must be lenient and sympathetic to the people. It should protect people and safeguard them. People feel that the government is harassing the people instead of protecting them." This was the summary of their representation.

The procession he saw in the morning, the representation he heard and the dharna of the women in red sarees highly upset Clee.

"Who are these women?" he asked the Tahshildar and Assistant Collector.

"They are widowed mendicants - nuns.... Sanyasinis," one of them mumbled, not able to tell the correct position.

"How many of them are there? Why have they come here?" the Collector asked loudly.

The Tahshildar never anticipated the situation. Instead of telling the number of women present, he remembered the census figures. "They are about one-thousand and odd of them in the taluk," he muttered.

Many of the widows were old. They were sweating and wiping the sweat with the end of the sarees. They looked tired. A few more women came and joined them. He thought 1000 of them would assemble there by the evening. The Collector was flabbergasted seeing the crowd.

"Why have they come? What is their complaint?" he asked.

"The Congressmen must have instigated them. All this is Gandhian mischief", the Tahshildar said.

"No no, ask them," the Collector went near them. "Why have you come?" he asked them in English. All of them were frightened. They covered their face by the sarees. But one woman got up and said in Kannada:

"Our Puranik is arrested. He used to offer consecrated ash to us."

"What is their complaint?" Clee asked.

A Christian officer mumbled: "It looks they have arrested their priest."

The Collector shouted to his subordinates.

"Look, you appear to be behaving in an high-handed way. Had I not told you to tackle the situation with care and caution and also tact. Why did you arrest the priest?"

"He did not pay revenue."

"Why did you arrest him? Work with tact. There are many who have not paid. Leaving them, you have held their priest first. You have provoked these nuns. Is this the way you run the administration?"

"No sir, we thought when the priest is taken to task others will pay."

"Nonsense, you have created a situation by which people will revolt. These nuns are helpless people. Even they have revolted. No, I can't bear this. I shall go to Sirsi right now. Pack up, pack up everything, quick," Clee ordered his servants and went in. The processionist widows shouted slogans in shrill voice and dispersed. The Assistant Collector shedding tears, pleaded with the Collector that he would handle the situation with care and implored that the Collector might kindly take food and take rest. The Saheb agreed to take food. But he had no appetite for eating. He was restless. He went in and stretched himself. Though a *pankha* was being pulled to keep the room cool, he felt the air was very hot. The Tahshildar had just gone out. All of a sudden something happened.

The Collector overheard a woman screaming from a distance. He came out and saw at the gate of the building a pregnant woman shouting at the police. She was accompanied by a 14 year girl. The faces of these two fair looking females had turned dark due to the exposure to the sun. "What is the matter?" the Collector enquired. The Assistant

Collector questioned her.

"You have arrested my husband. For the revenue dues of one-and-half rupee, you have confiscated our only milch cow. The bronze lamp near our God's image which was perpetually burning was extinguished and taken together with a bag full of cereals – all these things you confiscated. You are great sinners.... Now hang my husband and me too...," she shouted shivering all the while.

"What does she say?"

"Nothing, her husband, it looks, is arrested," the Assistant Collector said.

"Who is her husband?"

"Perhaps the same priest, who was arrested in the morning...," the Assistant Collector replied hesitatingly.

But the lady did not stop: "You have confiscated our milch cow. How can my month old child forego her food? The oil lamp in front of God's image, which was never extinguished, the *nandadeepa*, your men have taken away. They entered our prayer chamber with shoes on. Let your progeny perish for ever..."

"If you don't pay revenue dues Amma, all this follows....," the Assistant Collector tried to reason out. The Tahshildar who had perhaps gone out for a puff came back.

"Yes, we pay you revenue. But you don't protect us, you only tax us. Wild elephants ruined our crops. If pests ruin our crop and we reap nothing, how can we pay the taxes to you? You are a government who do not protect us. You want us to pay without your doing nothing for us?" the woman was haranguing.

"Don't tease her. You officers have done injustice to her. Otherwise such scenes would not have occurred. You are worthless people. Please send her back," saying these words the Collector withdrew, not being able to stand the woman who looked like a furious roaring lioness.

He had been highly disturbed mentally. "I will not stay here even for a minute. Let us start right now. Pack up, pack up everything," the Collector shouted.

☐☐

# Tax Collection Process

When Puranik was taken to Siddapur, Gulvadimam and Pundlik Shenoy went to his house from the back-door and consoled his wife and children. The Shanbhag and the police came to his house a little later. Even though there was a huge procession in protest against Puranik's arrest, the government was not perturbed by peoples' ire, and proceeded to confiscate Puranik's properties, and with a view to create panic in the minds of the people. Though what was due from Puranik was less than two rupees and that from his sister twenty rupees, they brought a fresh warrant to recover the amount. The milch cow of theirs, valued twenty rupees was evaluated at seven, and one bag full of paddy was valued as one rupee. They wanted some more items. A bronze lamp artistically designed, burning perpetually in the pooja room was valued at twelve annas. All this made Puranik's wife furious. In the burning sun, that pregnant lady walked to Siddapur. She met the Collector, took him to task fearlessly, and returned to Bilgi. Her visit to Siddapur was not known to Gulvadimam. Some teenaged volunteers had accompanied her and escorted her to the gates of the Circuit House. For her return journey she was provided with a bullock cart by Siddapur people.

When Gulvadimam heard all the news at the camp at night, he was surprised. That Puranik's wife, a highly conservative lady came out of her house and walked the distance in the scorching sun, caused great distress to him. He also thanked God for the role of the teenaged volunteers. More important was the behaviour of the Collector Clee.

"The victory of Satyagraha lies in the change of heart of men, officers and the government, Gandhiji has said. If an officer like Collector Clee was so much upset, that is the real victory of Satyagraha. This is the first victory of our campaign now," Gulvadimam said.

"All these high-handed acts are the handiwork of the lower officers only, you say. Has the Collector no role in it?" Ganapa Bhatta asked.

"At times such things have happened. The British officers at the top can be somewhat soft and kind, but our Indian officials behave like those 'more loyal than the king'. For example, in the Non-Cooperation Movement of 1921 there was an English Collector called Hague. He was the son of an Anglican priest who had settled down in Bangalore. He could speak Kannada well. During the Non-Cooperation Movement he did not pay much heed to many events of the movement. He did not arrest anybody. 'Ignore them', was his attitude as the movement was totally non-violent. But subordinate officers behaved with arrogance and high-handedness. Bedakani Chauda Nayak was arrested without the Collector's knowledge. Even the arrest of Timmappa Master took place due to the pressure of the Tahshildar of Sirsi.... So be it. Now, the confiscation campaign appears to be picking up speed. So we must conduct strong propaganda about the programme on the 4th at Siddapur. On that day police force of the whole taluk will be assembled. This will slow down the confiscations in the absence of the police in the villages. They intend to finish confiscations before the rainy season starts, that is their plan," said Gulvadimam.

"Why before rainy season?" asked Krishnaswamy.

"Movement from place to place is difficult. All rivers overflow."

"Today there were *japtis* in Lambapur region," Mahabal Hegde told. At Bijjala village, they came to Mahabalappa and asked him to pay two instalments. But Senior Hegde from Dodmane knew that they were coming to *japti* at Bijjala."

"Who told you this? Had Itagi Shiva come here in the morning?" Gulvadimam asked him.

"Not Shiva, his brother Hanama had come. Mahabalappa had removed all valuables from his residence. The Shanbhag came and demanded the land tax. 'Last year you had confiscated all vessels in our house. This year we could not have any crop. How can we pay now? Half the areca crop was destroyed by *koleroga* disease. Remaining half was damaged by monkeys. You have cancelled my gun licence. How am I to ward off the monkeys? Now what do I posses to pay you?' They searched the nooks and corners of his house. Nothing valuable except pottery vessels used for cooking were found. Then they entered neighbouring Shivamma's house. She is Sitaram Hegde's widow. There were two bags of paddy. They confiscated them saying they are from Mahabalappa's house. Actually the paddy belonged to Shivamma."

"That means Mahabalappa had kept his stock in Shivamma's house is their version, is it?" said Gulvadimam. "Last year in Hostota Subraya Hegde's case something similar happened. Six bags of pepper in his house were confiscated, attributing them to his cousin Narayana Hegde and they took away the bags."

"What happened later?" asked Krishnaswamy.

"What happened is immaterial. Both of them had participated in the movement. But these cousins were rank enemies. One did not see the face of the other. There was no chance of Narayana Hegde stocking the bags in his cousin's house. But people that had come for *japti* can't go empty-handed. If my cock is not available, take my neighbour's cock," said Gulvadimam. "Then what happened at Bijjala?" asked Gulvadimam.

"Shivamma insisted with the Shanbhag: 'Give me a receipt for what is confiscated.' They wrote a receipt in the name of Mahabalappa. Mahabalappa asserted loudly, 'This is not mine.' Then they issued a receipt in the name of Shivamma. 'This receipt is for the wet lands you own at Kelaginamane," they said. 'Kelaginamane land is not mine. Paramayya Hegde cultivates it. He holds it on *moolageni.* I have no obligation to pay tax on this land. It is he who has to pay revenue for the land. The *moolageni* rent of Rs. eight has not been paid by him this year,' Shivamma loudly grumbled. But they issued the receipt to her under duress. Then they called a servant of Mahabalappa and the police asked him to carry the bags of paddy. He refused to obey."

"Wonderful. I know him. He is called Phakira. He had come with me as my guide when I had gone there. He is Mahabalappa's bonded labourer. Last time he participated in Jungle Satyagraha. Then what happened next?" Gulvadimam asked.

"No, I won't come. If I come God will be displeased," Phakira said.

"If you don't come, 'we will arrest you' was the threat thrown at him."

"Arrest me, I will get government food," he replied.

"Wonderful."

"But they did not take the paddy bags. They arrested Mahabalappa and took him with them. Then his wife, five children and his widowed sister also joined him saying that they must be also arrested."

"Good good."

"Now look at this joke. Shivamma went to the Shanbhag and insisted that the paddy bags be taken away. 'Don't keep items confiscated in my house here," she said.

"I see, this is great," said Gulvadimam.

" 'No amma, I shall take it tomorrow,' the Shanbhag pleaded with her. 'Then take this receipt too. Only when you take the paddy bags, you issue me a receipt,' she insisted. Finally she tore the receipt and gave it to the Shanbhag. The police hit her twice with their lathi. 'Hit me, hit me, the British pay you salaries to hit women. Not thieves and dacoits', so saying Shivamma turned her back on them."

"Shabhas. They finally took Mahabalappa to Siddapur?"

"No, there lies the fun. They took Mahabalappa to Itgi and made him sit in the house of Itgi Shanbhag. Mahablappa's family members also sat there. At 7.30 p.m., they released them all."

"Including Mahabalappa?"

"That is what I am telling you Gulvadimam. Mahabalappa's family had not taken food since morning. On their release Dodmane Hegde took them to his house in a bullock cart."

"This is really wonderful. Krishna Bhatta, please prepare a report of what has happened this morning at Bilgi and Siddapur, and prepare six copies of it. Over there in that bag, there is paper, pencil, carbon paper etc. Include reports of what Phakira has narrated also in it. Tonight you must prepare it. Are you tired?"

"No no, it is only eleven in the night now. I shall complete it as you keep talking," Krishnaswamy said.

"Prepare three copies in Kannada and three in English. Kannada copies are to be sent to Bangalore *Vishwa Karnataka* and *Tainad* and one to Hubli, *Taruna Karnataka*."

"*Taruna Karnataka* has been closed down. Enough if you send the report to the Bangalore papers," said Ganapa Hegde.

"English reports may be sent to *Bombay Chronicle*, *Free Press Journal* in Bombay and *The Hindu* of Madras," said Gulvadimam.

"Unless you type it, they won't publish it," Mahabala Hegde said.

"Well and good if they publish. Last year the news from Bardoli was fully covered by the Bombay papers. Our news, even though typed and sent was not published by them. Anyway, if you send it ten times, at least once they will publish. Special news of the type we send, they do not publish. Reports of routine meetings and processions, only are published," Gulvadimam said.

"That is not a big thing," Mahabala Hegde said. "Year before last when I had been to Dharasana Salt Satyagraha, I went to Surat you see. On the first floor of the building there was a public meeting. About 120 persons were present. More than that number could not be accommodated in the hall. Next day when I saw the report in Bombay they had covered it with a double column heading. Our meetings here, far bigger than those, are attended by two to three thousand. It was too small a show for Surat, a district headquarters. Ours are minor centres. However huge our programmes are, they go unreported."

"Who works to get newspaper publicity? Today Shivamma demonstrated unprecedented gallantry. She has not done it expecting it will be publicised in *Bombay Chronicle*?" said Ganapa Bhatta.

"At what time Hanama met you?" Gulvadimam asked him.

"At eight and three quarters at Bilgi. He came riding a cycle. 'We have not received bulletins, please send them,' he said. I sent him to Mudlagiri Ram Pai. There is likelihood of *japtis* taking place at Kelaginamane, Vajagondu, Danamavu and Talakere; they are immediate targets, was the news to be conveyed to you, according to Dodmane Hegde," he said.

"Is it? Then Kelaginamane is near Bijjala. They may start from Kelaginamane itself, tomorrow," Gulvadimam anticipated.

"Kelaginamane Nagesh Hegde has signed the pledge," Ganapa Bhatta reminded.

"Signed of course. But how firm are they? Theirs is a large household, Gulvadimam," said Mahabala Hegde.

"No, there are no determined people like them. Nagesh Hedge had resigned his Village Headmanship in 1921 and he is very firm. Last year he courted arrest and served jail term by undertaking Jungle Satyagraha," Gulvadimam said.

"Why did he resign Village Headmanship?" Ganapa Bhatta asked.

"You don't know the Coimbatore Saheb's episode? Dodmane Narayan Hegde boycotting Assistant Commissioner Coimbatore?"

"I have heard, but do not know the details."

"A boy called Coimbatore had stayed and grown up in Narayana Hegde's father's house. His father from Tamil area had come wandering (*deshavari*) and was staying in the house of Narayana Hegde. Narayana Hegde's father had the boy educated. Later he joined government service and rose to be an Assistant Commissioner. Earlier he was posted at Dharwad. Later he came to Sirsi."

"Yes, I have heard that Coimbatore was highly embarrassed."

"That is what I am narrating. On his circuit visit, he came and stayed at Narayana Hegde's house. 'I am going to Bilgi. It will be late while I return. There is a meeting at Bilgi,' Narayan Hegde told the officer. 'What meeting?' the Officer questioned. 'Congress meeting,' Narayana Hegde replied. 'No, do not attend Congress meetings,' the Officer ordered Narayana Hegde. 'Who are you to order me?' Narayana Hegde retorted. 'I am Assistant Commissioner. Don't join Congress,' the Officer said. 'You are an officer, in your office. Not in my house. Here your powers won't operate,' Narayana Hegde replied. 'I am an Officer wherever I am. You don't go and you should not go,' the Officer said. 'You had eaten our food, grown up in our house, and now you want to show your powers to me? You come to our house only if you are the son of Coimbatore Nanjundayya. If you act as Assistant Commissioner, do not come to our house in that capacity. Before I return home in the night, you must vacate my house. Don't demonstrate your Sahebgiri in my house. Do you understand?' So saying Narayana Hegde left for Bilgi in his horse carriage. As some serious issues were discussed at Bilgi, Narayana Hegde was in a bad temper. By the time he returned home, the officer had finished his supper and was chewing betel. Coimbatore it looks had not taken Narayana Hegde's warning seriously because from boyhood days they had grown up together. 'Had I not told you to vacate my house? Why are you still here? Get out, Get out,' Hegde shouted, and asked his servants to throw out all his belongings. Saheb was furious. 'I will teach you a lesson,' he warned Hegde and started towards Itgi with his retinue. 'Having grown up in our house, having partaken food with us, do we deserve to be taught lessons by you? It is our mistake that we fed milk to a serpent like you,' Narayana Hegde told the officer."

"Soon all Village headmen, Patels, it looks resigned, is it?"

"Yes, let me tell you the whole story. The Officer had, it appears threatened Narayana Hegde that he will have him arrested. 'I shall see you can't wield your power here,' Hegde replied. He sent all his men late in the night, and before dawn 80 Patels in the taluk decided to resign. Coimbatore became helpless. Wherever he went nobody came to receive him. At Itgi, nobody offered water or food to him. The next day he faced boycott in every village on the way. That is why Collector Hague was very careful. It was at that time Kelaginamane Nagesh Hegde had resigned. Since then, he is a staunch follower of Congress."

Seated in a corner, having heard this story, Krishnaswamy started shedding tears of joy. Such important events had occurred in this district. But they never came to light, he wondered.

"Now Mahabala, you be here in the camp tomorrow. Our men from Hostota, Neralamane and Huvinamane camps will be coming. Tell them that on the 4$^{th}$ they must come to Chandraghatgi's courtyard by twelve o'clock. I am telling you of Gandhi Day programme. No male should remain at home. Tell them that from every camp they should fetch 100 people. Myself, Krishnabhatta, (Krishna Bhatta, are you hearing me?) and Ganapa Bhatta, we three will start at six in the morning and reach Kelaginamane. For three days, Krishna Bhatta, you be there. Now you are in the battle field. You know our methods. You have to direct people. Whatever you want to wear during the next two to three days, I mean clothing etc., you take with you. Having not had a shave for the past three days, and got your body tanned, you have become a rustic. Tomorrow we start at six," Gulvadimam said.

"O yes," said Krishnaswamy. But the words 'you have to direct people' created a feeling of rapture, and also fright in Krishnaswamy. He felt that his heartbeat stopped for a while!

"If your report is ready, enclose them in covers. There are revenue stamps in the bags. Affix them. These revenue stamps are from Bhatkal tahshildar's office: Covers, carbon sheets and paper are also from there. If we affix service stamps, C.I.D. will have no suspicion. There will be no intercepting and censoring. See Mahabala, these must be sent through Chauda to Siddapur tomorrow and handed over to the cleaner of Sagar bus asking him to post it from Sagar. Only from Sagar, not from other places," Gulvadimam said.

"How did you get these service stamps?" Krishnaswamy was inquisitive.

"We have our own men in government departments. Somebody from Bhatkal taluk office supplies it. Stencil ink we use is also from there. The government servants sympathetic to us are in considerable number. Many government decisions even before they are implemented reach us. You will know about these sources soon."

"Tomorrow night you will not be here?" Mahabala Hegde asked Gulvadimam.

"Tomorrow night I will come. Let Ganapa Bhatta stay with Krishna Bhatta. Tomorrow Heggere Ira will be here. Ask him to stay here. In case Chauda goes to Siddapur, you may want somebody here. Nagesh Prabhu's brother, Narna, also will be here. If he comes, retain him for the whole day. There can be *japtis* at Bilgi. Pundlik takes care of all that."

Chauda came running and announced that somebody is coming

from Siddapur side.

"It is twelve now. Let us see who it is," saying this, Gulvadimam went out. Two young men came.

"It is I, Mhalappa, Gulvadimam."

"Arre, you Mhalappa, what news," Gulvadimam asked anxiously.

"This evening at 7.30, Gopal Shenoy was arrested."

"Is it? Arrested? Where?"

"In Siddapur at Durgappa Shanbhag's house. They were talking about today's developments. At 7.30, he and Ibrahim set out from the house. It was dark. The police who came on cycles arrested them. Gopal Shenoy had not moved even 20 steps from the house," said Mhalappa.

"Where is he now?"

"In Siddapur lock-up. Durgappa Shanbhag wanted me to inform this to you. We two came, double-riding on a cycle. Near Bhuvanagiri the cycle's tyre punctured. We left the cycle at the temple priest's house and came."

"O God, the Third Leader of our taluk is arrested. This is bad. He should have been free at least till 4th. Tomorrow I shall reach Lambapur. Ask Dodmane Nagesh Hegde to take charge. Let us take this as a challenge…."

"Who is the person arrested?" Krishnaswamy enquired.

"The same person we met at Bilgi, Gopal."

"Pundlik's brother?"

"Yes, The, same person. Now, Mhalappa and Bhaira, you stay here tonight. I will leave early in the morning. Now what about your night meal?"

"Night meal…." Mhalappa said hesitatingly. "It is half past-twelve now. Don't worry."

"No, no. Shankara has gone to bed. Do not awaken him. Chauda, see in the kitchen, in a tin there is beaten rice and jaggery. Give them a mug full of water. Krishna Bhatta? Your report is ready? Write at the bottom the latest news: 'The Third Leader of Siddapur taluk, Gopal Shenoy of Bilgi is arrested today'. Mahabala, send those covers with Mhalappa. Do not send Chauda to Siddapur. Mhalappa, these covers must be given to the cleaner of Sagar bus to be posted at Sagar. You know our method. I had asked Naga Bhatta to send twenty-five rupees to this camp for the expenses. He need not come here for that purpose. We shall collect it on the 4th when we come to Siddapur. For the present we do not require cash. Arre! Did you hear the sound Krishna Bhatta? It is the King of Malnad!" Gulvadimam said. It was the sound of a tiger's growl, heard from not far away.

"Is it a tiger?" Krishnaswamy asked.

"Yes, tiger. Not a mouse. It is on the bank of the stream. Tomorrow morning do not go to the stream when it is dark. Manage with the water stored here," Gulvadimam advised him.

"How did these people come here?"

"They came from the opposite direction. They could have come across the tiger. Even on the roads tigers roam."

"This is very dangerous. In case we come across the tiger tomorrow morning what are we to do?"

"What to do? Shake hands with it. Invite him for the Siddapur programme on the 4th. You are frightened? Then I will call the King Tiger to be here and introduce you to him." All in the camp laughed heartily.

The lamplight was made to flicker. All went to sleep. The events of the day looked like incidents that have occurred in the course of a week to Krishnaswamy. The young men came from Siddapur in the darkness of the night. Their valour, fearlessness and devotion made Krishnaswamy feel proud of them.

□□

# Sarvatra Gandhi

Having got up early and walking seven or eight miles, by seven o'clock Gulvadimam and the other two reached Kelaginamane stream. From there he sent word to Kelaginamane Nagesh Hegde. Ganapa Bhatta saw a servant of Nagesh Hegde in a field on the way, and asked him to inform Nagesh Hegde that Gulvadimam has come. He was told to approach Nagesh Hegde from the back-door. Ganapa Bhatta waited there.

After 20 minutes, Nagesh Hegde's brother Ramakrishna came. "My brother has gone to Vajagodu. He will soon come back. Today they are visiting Vajagodu and our place for *japti.* My brother wanted to inform Vajagod people in advance," he said.

"How have you prepared yourself?", Gulvadimam asked the visitor.

"What preparation? The valuables in all the three houses have been taken away and hidden. Our Kite-Eyed was always watching us. Without his knowledge we have done the needful."

"Is it? Then good. You are Nagesh Hegde's brother, Ramachandra?" Gulvadimam asked.

"No, Ramakrishna is my name."

"Ramakrishna, where is your brother?"

"He has gone to Vajagodu to warn people about the *japti* party's visit. He will be back in an hour".

"You have come from Bilgi?" Ramakrishna asked.

"Yes, now we go to Bijjala and will be back here in an hour. If your brother comes, ask him to wait here. At what time the Japti party is expected?"

"Yesterday they had been to Bijjala. Mabalappa may not be there. You please wait here. I will arrange to send breakfast for you."

"At Bijjala I want to meet at least Shivamma. I will send Krishna Bhatta and Ganapa Bhatta with you. Ganapa Bhatta, does anybody know you here?"

"Your Kite-Eye knows me, who is the Shanbhag here?"

"Kyadgi Narayanappa. He stays at Siddapur".

"He may not know me. But your Kite-Eye Patel Sambajja might know me", Ganapa Bhatta said.

"Then Ganapa Bhatta, you don't go. Take this Krishna Bhatta with you, Ramakrishna. Tell people that he is your relative from Sagar. Let him be there to help you. Krishna Bhatta, you do not talk to anybody, especially the officials. Just guide these people if need be. You take your baggage with you. Later I will send necessary message on my return from Bijjala. Cheer you."

Krishnaswamy accompanying Ramakrishna walked across a path full of ups and downs, and after walking on the sides of sugarcane crop, came to a spot where there were only four houses. The spot was Kelginamane.

"How many houses are there?", Krishnaswamy enquired on the way.

"Ours is one, another is of our cousin Paramayya Hegde, and the third is that of Parvati Hegde, a widow. All of us have signed No-Tax pledge. Near our house lives another cousin, Chungadi Sambajja. We call him Kite-Eye. He is the Patel of our area. He took over the post after my brother resigned. He is a great intriguer. We have a common roof for our old family house. They try to overhear all the talk in our house."

"How did you remove the valuables from your house?"

"All that we had planned for 15 days. During the midnight we removed the items one at a time. They were vigilant, but we did not let them know."

They reached their house. The huge house had two parts. To the right side was Patel Sambajja's house, to the left there was Nagesh Hegde's house. Ramakrishna took Krishnaswamy to a cell which was dark and introduced Krishna Bhatta to his brothers Subraya and Narayana: "Tell the people he is our guest from Sagar, on a visit to Gokarna."

In the meanwhile boys from Patel Sambajja's house conducted two sorties round the house to know who the new comer was. Krishnaswamy was served on a plantain leaf bananas and *happala* of jackfruit.

"We have shifted our metal vessels. Now we cook only in earthen vessels. We have kept here hidden only some metal cups to drink. Let us wait till the boys from Sambajja's house go," said Narayana. Krishnaswamy removed his watch from his waist band. It was 8.15.

From afar they heard slogan shouting by boys, "Mahatma Gandhi Ki Jai."

"The party has come. Ambakka, you leave. Come only after I send a word. Even if it is late in the afternoon, you be there," Ramakrishna told a lady present there.

"Who are these boys shouting," Krishnaswamy asked.

"These are volunteers from the nearby hamlets. Our Monkey Brigade has been instructed to shout slogans when the party arrives," Subraya said.

A girl came running and told them:

"Sambajja is coming with the police."

"Where are they?" Ramakrishna asked her.

"They are crossing the stream."

"Let them come. You be here. Now don't go again," Ramakrishna told her.

Dogs started barking loudly. Now the party came near the hamlet. Boys started shouting slogans and sang a song in chorus. "Gandhiye Gandhi Sarvatra Gandhi" in Kannada ('It is Gandhi, Gandhi everywhere'). Krishnaswamy became nervous. Now he was in the battle, face to face with the enemy! Bugle was blown. "But what am I to do actually," he was wondering. "Satyagraha is not the weapon of the coward," he remembered Gandhiji's words. "If I am to lose my heart, what will others do?"

A constable with a gun in hand stood in front of the house and another stood behind the house as guards. Ramakrishna told this to Krishnaswamy. "Have they come to arrest me, knowing of my coming here? How to escape from here?" He remembered various incidents of workers having escaped when they were surrounded. Behind Parvati's house there was one male and behind Paramayya's house another male was standing, but they are not constables, but *Ugranis,* he was told. "They have put sentries, perhaps only to arrest me," was Krishnaswamy's feeling.

Other members of the party were the Police Jamadar, and two other officials. Perhaps, the Sub-Inspector and Shanbhag were on the Chavadi (platform) of Sambajja's house. They were having breakfast, Krishnaswamy was informed. After half-an-hour the Shanbhag came near Nagesh Hegde's house and questioned whether Nagesh Hegde was there. Nobody replied.

Then Narayan went out. "Namaskar Shanbhagre, Anna is not here. What do you want please?" he said.

"Nagesh Hegde is not in? Where has he gone? Is Ramakrishna present?"

"He is there, I shall call him."

"Now all responsibilities are on my shoulders. What am I to do?" Krishnaswamy was worried.

Both Ramakrishna and Narayana came out.

"Come, the Revenue Inspector is calling you", the Shanbhag said. They went to the Chavadi of Sambajja.

"Nagesh Hegde is not here?" one officer questioned.

"He went out early in the morning, it is time he may come," said Ramakrishna. Krishnaswamy was overhearing all this.

"You have no intention to pay the land revenue? Notice has been issued to you twice."

"My brother has to speak about that, he will come now."

"He must have hid himself somewhere."

"What is the gain in hiding oneself?"

"Who knows," the officer said. "If you do not pay you know what happens? Is this a Gandhi village? You have taught all boys to sing 'Gandhiye Gandhi Sarvatra Gandhi.'" All boys in the courtyard started singing in chorus 'Gandhiye Gandhi.'

"You monkeys, get away," Sambajja threatened them. A constable standing in front of Nagesh Hegde's house tried to threaten them. One boy told the constable: "O Polisappa, please shoot us." 'Bolo Bharat Mataki' he said. All boys said 'Jai'." The constable lifted the gun to beat them, using it as a lathi. The boys ran away and then shouted slogans loudly. The constable picked up a piece of firewood and chased them. From a distance, a boy loudly addressed the constable: "Polisappa, you don't know how to shoot? Please shoot. Let us hear the sound *doom doom.*" Another boy said. "The gun has no cartridge to shoot." The officers on the chavadi also laughed. One boy started singing loudly in Kannada.

"*O motherland, let us serve at your feet,*
*With great pleasure,*
*we give our lives for your comfort,*
*Let us not be deterred by the gun shot or lathi hit*
*We stand erect and give our*
*Lives for you.*"

All boys loudly said: "Let us not be deterred by gun shot or lathi hit, Let us give our lives for you."

As the chorus ended, one boy spoke loudly: "Chandi Chamundi what is your demand?" Another boy said: "If you are a valiant male, sacrifice your head."

One officer could not control his laughter. "What are all things they have been taught, these young boys! They do not understand what they sing," he said.

"Who follows the rules Saheb? Non-payment of land tax is sedition. The government can do anything. This village folk do not understand it. They dance to the tunes of Congress leaders. Has Gandhi paid the land revenue? It seems around his Ashram there is land measuring hundreds of acres. Let him stop paying the tax," Chungadi Sambajja said.

"Why not? Year before last, when Gandhiji refused to pay tax, his

Navjeevan press was seized. They wanted to auction it. As there were no bidders at Ahmedabad, they sent the press items to Bombay. There too nobody came to bid. Later after the Gandhi-Irvine Pact, the material was taken back to Sabarmati Ashram and returned to the Ashram people, saying '*Dammayya,* please take it back'," Narayan said.

"I see! You have all the information," an officer said. This angered Sambajja.

"Look Narayana, we have not called you to get all this information from you. Why do you say all this?"

Narayana was nonplussed for a while. "You had called us to know whether our Anna (elder brother) is present. Anna is not here. You called us to enquire about the Land tax. Anna has to answer. Our job is over. Why should we talk things we are not expected to? Sahebs, we take leave of you. Namaskara." Both the brothers stood up.

"No no, don't go. It is not so simple. Wait a little while," the officer said.

"Now the Patel has ordered us. Why should we disobey his orders?" Narayana said.

"No. I order you. Now you stop," the officer said.

"What is the use of ordering? We do not obey the orders of the British Government. You are not our rulers," Narayana replied laughingly.

"What are you talking? If the government is not there, where will you be? Is there safety for you if police and government are not there? If thieves and dacoits come, attack you physically and loot you, who takes care for you? Where will be peace and order?"

"Where is that peace Sabeb? Last year at Herur and Hulimane dacoits looted so many houses. What did your government do? Have you apprehended any dacoit? Again last year elephants came and destroyed our crops and destroyed all our plants. What did the government do? People who come to collect land-tax, do they help us to protect our crops? In the course of last 20 years, there is an increase of forest area by 15 per cent. Population has dwindled by 12 per cent. Not being able to bear the pinpricks of the government, harassment of the Forest Department, people have run away. Many have died of malaria. Is there peace? What peace? Peace of the graveyard?"

"You must tell all this to your Congress leader, mister. What is the use of telling us. Gandhiji has thousands of soldiers of Seva Dal. Frontier Gandhi has lakhs of Red Shirts."

"Yes Sir, we shall tell them. We will pay Land Tax also to them. You please do not demand it," Narayana told them sarcastically.

"I see, this fellow is well-informed. Wonderful!" the officer said.

"You can call us fools, or bloody fools, we don't mind. Now we move," said Narayana and the brothers were about to leave.

"No, don't go", the officer said. "Otherwise, we have to arrest you."

"Saheb, this country itself is a jail. What if we are in or out of it? Last year I had been imprisoned for six months. In our country to be in jail is more comfortable. We did not get a fair yield from lands even to help us to have two square meals a day. And if we pay Land Tax, we can't eat anything in the rainy season," Ramakrishna said. By then the singing and shouting of boys stopped. A girl came running and announced "Doddappa has come."

"Is this Mr.Nagesh Hegde? Come, come here on the Chavadi," said one officer. By then Narayana and Ramakrishna were climbing down the Chavadi. "Are these your younger brothers? They were quarrelling with us," the officer continued.

"Quarrel is verbal, is it not? There might not have been any physical scuffle," Nagesh Hegde said. "You have come to collect Land Tax?" he continued.

"Yes you have to pay two instalments. You have received our two notices?"

"I myself delivered it," the Ugrani said.

"We have received the notices. But we don't pay the Tax."

"Look here Mr.Hegde. Don't take hasty steps. In case you do not pay, we have to resort to *Japti*. Your household goods, lands, your cattle, garden, all these will be forfeited. For disobeying the government, you will be jailed. Please think. Think of your wife and children. Your brothers are young men and hot headed. You cannot behave like them."

"Sir, Inspector saheb, we have fully thought of all this. We are soldiers of the country. Gandhiji is our captain. We follow his orders. Even if our children have to beg, we don't mind. We are Brahmins and asking for alms is a part of our tradition. We gave up our brahminhood and took to agriculture. This Land Tax, this Chauthayi, etc. are a torture to us."

"See Mr.Nagesh Hegde, the British government has the police force and military. Can your Gandhi and Congressmen win against them? Even nations like Germany, Austria, the powerful Turkeystan have bitten dust in the last war."

"Sir, this is the right point. Vishwamitra was king. He had four-divisions (Chaturanga) of the army. Chariots, elephants, horses and foot soldiers he had. With this vast army, he fought against Vasishtha. What had Vasishtha? His own weapon was his Danda Kamandala. Danda Kamandala had stored energy earned by his penance. Vishwamitra's army had to bite dust before his power of penance. Similarly Gandhiji's truth, non-violence and Satyagraha are his powers of penance. The British armed power has to bow its head, and Gandhiji's power of penance will win. This is hundred per cent true," Nagesh Hedge said.

"This fellow has been inspired. Are you an *arthadari* (interpreter) in Yakshagana?" the officer asked.

"Yes. That is not the issue now? Is it not because of Gandhiji's penance that the British signed an agreement with him last year? It resulted in Gandhi-Irvine Pact and Gandhiji went to London. The Mahatma was taken to the palace and King George shook hands with him with honour. The Mahatma had not gone wearing suit and boot. He went there wearing a *panche* and *uttariya.* In Aden, Egypt and France lakhs of people thronged to honour him. Why has America invited him?"

"Yes, Mahatma is a great Tapasvi. In 1920, he said he would get swaraj to India in 12 months. Now 12 years have passed. Even if 120 years pass Swaraj won't dawn. This is an empire where the sun will never set. Is your Mahatma going to set the sun?" another Revenue Inspector asked him.

"Sir, there have been many kings who ruled and vanished. Many empires also similarly vanished. What is permanent? If this is the empire where sun will never set, what was the need for lakhs of white soldiers and our Indian soldiers to die in the World War? The empire whose sun will never set had its financial power crumbling, and they had to take gold worth crores from our country. In the last four months, they have taken gold worth thirty-six and odd crores of rupees from our land. The news had appeared in the papers. It is said we produce gold worth 18 crores every year. If all gold in our country is exhausted, then at least the British government will turn bankrupt. Will the sun set at least then?"

"See, Mr.Nagesh Hegde, the whole world is facing economic depression now. People have no money. The industries in England have closed down."

"Yes, Gandhiji told us 'Charkha Chala Chalake, lenge swarjya lenge.' We launched boycott of foreign goods movement. Two years ago our import from Britain was worth 103 crores. Last year it fell to 70 crores. In Lancashire, cloth mills have been closed down. Labourers have been unemployed. 'Your boycott movement in India has created this army of unemployed in Lancashire,' people told Gandhi in England. Did not the British tell this to Gandhiji when he was in England? Now the sun has started setting. If we don't pay Tax, that sun is sure to set totally."

"Why waste time by talking to him? He looks to be a chatter box....Let us do our duty," one officer told the other in English.

"No, let us hear his case. It is funny."

"By lending ears to his arguments should we go empty handed? What about our duty?"

"Sir, you please perform your duty. In case you want to undertake *japti* please do it," Nagesh Hegde said.

"You appear to have shifted your household goods elsewhere. That is why you boldly tell us to undertake *japti*?" the Shanbhag said.

"Dear Shanbhag, your Patel and I have a common roof. Even if a pin is dropped in our house, he hears its sound. Even if a fly leaves our house he will know. What items can we shift without his knowledge?

Last year arecanut crop was destroyed by nut disease. This year too it is the same situation. The monkey menace destroyed what was spared on the tree top. We requested for the *tahqub* (postponement) of Tax collection. For the application we sent, a reply came saying that we had not applied with two rupee revenue stamp attached to the application. We sold what metal vessels we had and purchased rice for our daily use. But do you leave us because we don't possess anything in our house? You have super-weapons (*Brahmastras*) in your arsenal. If the government arrested Puranik at Bilgi yesterday, you can arrest us today or tomorrow. You can as well forfeit our house or land," said Nagesh Hegde.

"You know all this?" one officer asked.

"Who says we don't know? We are not innocent children. Ready to sacrifice our house, life, family, and everything we have joined the movement, having full faith in us, Gandhiji has gone to jail."

The Monkey Brigade started its slogans. They started singing "Gandhi, it is Gandhi everywhere." (*Gandhiye Gandhi sarvatra Gandhi*).

□□

# Seizure!

"Climb up the attic. It is dark there. Bhima, go to our house and bring a lighted lantern. Wait for some time, dig the ground in the *pooja* room. Take this pick-axe," Patel Sambajja was issuing instructions. The Ugrani should not enter the *pooja* room, was the strong objection of the ladies. They were dragged out by the police. Narayana Hegde was furious. He was knotting his long pigtail. Krishnaswamy silently signalled him to be calm. All goods and items found in the nooks and corners were put upside down during the search. After the search in Nagesh Hegde's house, they could lay hands on two-and half seers of rice kept for food and two brass mugs. Those were the only items worth confiscating. Two cows that had gone to hills for grazing were identified and arranged to be brought down by Patel Sambajja. According to their evaluation all the items valued Rs. 31 only! The Land revenue, Chautai and other dues totalled Rs.118. A receipt was issued for Rs. 31. The cows were tied in front of Sambajja's house.

Next, the party went to Parvati Hegde's house. A brass vessel was kept to cook rice on the oven in the kitchen. The half baked rice with water was ordered to be emptied by the Ugrani. The Ugrani emptied the vessel in the front yard. The whole house was searched. One mug and two drinking tumblers of brass were located, and nothing else.

"Where is your cow? It is not in the cowshed," Patel prompted the

Shanbhag to ask the question.

"Yesterday night somebody has stolen it. The rope with which I had bound it, itself has been cut. I wanted to complain to our Patel. He was also not to be seen in the morning," Parvati replied.

Next they entered the *Pooja* room. Near the small image there was a small tin container. They opened it despite Parvati strongly protesting that it was money reserved (*hundi*) for God Tirupathi Venkatesha. It contained silver two-anna coins. "During every festival and function in our house, I put one coin as reserve for God," she said. Despite her protest not to touch it they counted the money and totally seven-and-half rupees were found. "The person who touches the *hundi* money, will have their progeny destroyed," Parvati cursed. All items including the cash in the tin box were calculated and the amount came to nine rupees and one anna. The balance dues were announced to be rupees three and half anna and a receipt was issued. "The money in the name of God should not be taken," Parvati repeatedly protested. But none paid heed. The half-baked rice thrown in front yard was being eaten by the crows. "The *pitrs* (departed elders) of the British government are satisfied. Crows are partaking the *pinda*," (rice ball offered during obsequies), a boy said loudly. The sub-inspector stared at him, opening his eyes wide. The boy also stared at the sub-inspector and made circuitous jumps (*dhigana* as done in Yakshagana). The Monkey Brigade started slogan shouting.

The last house was of Paramayya Hegde. There too there was nothing valuable to lay hands on. Sambajja ordered the inner chamber floor of the house to be dug to the depth of four feet. There, all his brass and copper vessels were found buried. Sambajja had knowledge of this act of Paramayya. Vessels worth about seventy rupees were valued at rupees sixty. Dues from Paramayya were fifty-nine rupees. They wrote a receipt for full collection of the dues. The vessels were shifted to a room in Sambajja's house and the room was locked. Losing domestic vessels caused much distress to Paramayya's wife and daughters. Each vessel in the house had its own dear memory to the women. They went into the house and started weeping. By then the confiscating party had finished its job at Kelaginamane. It was noon.

They had a hearty lunch at Sambajja's house.

Krishnaswamy, Narayana and Subraya went to Paramayya's house. "The brass *uruvali* (a round vessel) and water pitcher was given to me by my mother. The huge *hande* of copper was bought at Gokarna *jatra* this year. 'Don't bury them in the house,' I pleaded with my husband repeatedly. He did not listen to me. Now everything is gone. Here in our house even walls have ears," Shivamma wept loudly.

"What is this Shivattige? Having performed a holy pilgrimage, does anybody calculate the total expenses? Though no items were found in our house, we have not escaped. They will issue orders to forfeit our lands and areca garden. You at least have your dues settled. You had decided firmly in advance not to pay. What is the point in feeling distressed now?" said Narayana.

"Attige (sister-in-law), last year Vajgod Ganapayya's bullocks were forfeited. But he has joined No-Tax campaign again. Ganapayya's wife Bhagirathamma herself said that they will not pay," Subraya said.

Krishnaswamy, being shy to speak to women, spoke loudly addressing all. "Maharaja Harishchandra gave up his whole realm for the sake of Truth. His wife Chandramati gave up the palace to honour the truthful words of her husband and suffered so much. These people lived in jungles and suffered – all for Truth's sake. This sacrifice is similar."

Shivamma stopped weeping. "Year before last, my husband participated in Jungle Satyagraha and underwent a three-month jail term. On return, he participated in picketing in front of liquor shop and was sentenced for one-month term. Our daughter Rukku's marriage could not be arranged. Two most likely marriage proposals we missed. Having a grown up girl being kept at home without marriage, to which hell will we go? If he is imprisoned again, marriage will be further postponed," Shivamma poured out her anguish. Young Rukku blushed when she heard the talk of her marriage.

"Shivattige, now do not go on worrying. Be bold. All children are hungry. You Rukku, get up. In our house they have spread leaves to take lunch…," said Narayana.

Rukku stood up. She was fourteen year old, well grown girl. While going out, she threw a smile at Krishnaswamy. Haviks are generally fair complexioned. This girl was very fair. Weeping had turned her eyes and face all the more red and she looked more beautiful to Krishnaswamy.

"All of you go for food… where is Shankra? Call Shankra," Rukku told a boy.

"Shankaranna has gone to Vajagod with Monkey Brigade," the girl replied.

"Gone to Vajagod? He has not taken his meal," Shivamma said.

"Ganappa, Sheshanna, Parama, all went to Vajagod. Shankaranna joined them," the girl replied.

The matter was clear. They heard that the *japti* party was going to Vajagod. The Monkey Brigade reached the hamlet in advance to welcome them!

When he heard that the *Japti* party had left after food, Krishnaswamy also felt that he should go to Vajagod. But as there were no persons known to him, police might identify him as an outsider and apprehend him. Sambajja might be knowing that he is a guest who had come to Nagesh Hegde's house. Sambajja had also gone to Vajagod. Gulvadimam had said that he would reach that place later.

He just peeped into the kitchen of Paramayya's house. The five-feet deep excavation was a heart-rending scene. It wore a ghastly look. Similarly they had dug the *pooja* room in Nagesh Hegde's house.

"Krishnabhava, have you taken your bath?" asked Narayana.

"Yes," said Krishnaswamy. It was embarrassing for him to take a bath near the well without a sacred thread on.

By then, a youth came running. On the way to Vajagod there was a two-acre wet land of Bettada Parvatamma. Namadhari Huliya was her tenant. Sambajja took the *japti* party to the garden. In case he pays the land revenue of the garden, a Patta will be issued in Huliya's name, said the Revenue Inspector, trying to persuade and coax Huliya. Sambajja also tried to convince him: "Pay rupees thirteen and seven annas. You will be the owner of this property. There is no need for you to pay rent in future to Parvati. The land will be yours."

"Why do you teach such greed to me? We are cultivating this land from my grandfather's days. We pay our rent. That great mother, Mahatayi, does not make any demand on us. She treats us as her children. Once when elephants destroyed the crops, she herself donated us two *kolagas* of paddy. The Mahatayi is like our mother who has given birth to us."

"All that is old story Huliya; now those times have gone. Things have changed. In case you don't have money, I will lend you cash. *Patta* will be in your name. Follow my advice. Goddess of wealth Mahalakshmi is knocking at your door. Don't kick her out," Sambajja tried to convince him.

"No Patelsaheb, no. I do not want such Mahalakshmi earned by unfair methods. Though we are poor, God has given us sturdy arms. We toil, sweat and earn. We do not open the door to Mahalakshmi who comes to us unjustly….," Huliya said firmly.

"Look Huliya, if you do not pay Revenue and your Dhani (Owner) also does not pay, the land you cultivate will be forfeited and will be auctioned. Neither you nor your Dhani will have the land. Without the land, you may have to beg… This house where you live will also have to be vacated by you. People who purchase this land by auction will come to live on this land."

"Let anything happen Patelsaheb. Let *paramatma's* will prevail. If it is written on my forehead that I have to be a beggar, who can prevent it? Who can order me that a house in which we are living from my grandfather's days will have to be vacated?"

"You say what is written in your forehead will come true, without paying Land Rent. Take this money, have a receipt. The land in which you are a tenant will be yours. You become the owner, *Dhani,* master!" saying this Sambajja tried to pay silver coins to Huliya. Huliya went away from Sambajja and firmly said that he would not pay the Land Tax. The young man who had come narrated the whole story.

"Who is that Huliya, the hero, I must see him," Krishnaswamy said.

"Now you take food, and then we shall go," said Nagesh Hegde.

A boy came running and muttered something into his ears.

"Ask him to come here. Food is ready," Nagesh Hegde told the boy. The boy went running towards the stream.

"Gulvadimama has come. Reserve space for him to take food."

Krishnaswamy was wondering, 'What report I could present to Gulvadimama in case he asks me what all I did here. In what way I guided the movement? When the police dragged the women out of Nagesh Hegde's house, Narayana was furious. I simply signalled to him to be calm. This work could as well have been done by Subraya Hegde or Ramakrishna Hegde. I tried to console Paramayya's wife. Nothing more I did. How to conduct the movement, these people know fully well. There is nothing for me to guide them.'

Gulvadimama came. He discussed the events of the day with Nagesh Hegde. "After Vajagod, they might go to Danamavu. Today morning Dodmane Nagesh Hegde had visited the place. Talekere is just at a distance of a shout from there. There are only two houses. Now, it is 2.30 p.m. Now they may be at Vajagodu. There are three houses there. Manjayya is a loyalist. He is a disciple of Sambajja. Ganapayya is a strong guy. He is a cousin of Manjayya," Nagesh Hegde told him.

"Last year Ganapayya's house was to be forfeited together with their cattle being undervalued. But his wife argued with the officer and prevented forfeiture of the house. I was told," said Gulvadimam.

"Yes, he has five acres of garden land and two acres of wet land. He is a strong guy. His is maximum land tax. Another house there is his sister's, Timmayya Bhatta's wife. She has also signed the pledge. And on the way there is Huliya, I think you know of him?"

"Yes, boys told me about him on the way. It looks he refused to pay tax despite the officials promising him to give the *Patta* in his name. He is really great."

"Look at this Sambajja's antics. It looks he offered him a loan to pay the tax."

"This has happened many times. Year before last, in Ankola taluk, many Nadavar tenants were similarly coaxed to pay the rent and have the *Patta* in their names as the owner of the land refused to pay

Tax. But the whole Nadavar community was and is united and highly patriotic. Here this single Namadhari Huliya refusing to oblige the officials is creditable. Who has told him to do this? Who had thought that somebody will approach him with these ideas. It is really great. I want to meet him.", Gulvadimam said. Then he saw Krishnaswamy and said, "Hello Krishna Bhatta, what is your experience?"

"Very good experience Gulvadimam. But I had no role to play. People know how to face things. I am a passive onlooker."

"No, no, it is not like that. Your presence is a matter of solace to us. My brothers, our women were all full of courage because of your presence. Here is a person who is in the know of things they felt and took courage from you," Nagesh Hegde said. The importance of workers coming from outside was somewhat realised by Krishnaswamy.

All the cooking was done in the earthen pots. For drinking water the small flat cups made of plantain leaves were used. Krishnaswamy found it difficult to drink water from those cups. "Till the time this movement is over copper and bronze vessels will have to be kept hidden. When guests like you come we feel very uneasy over these things," Nagesh Hegde told Krishnaswamy.

"I am not a guest. Persons like me are soldiers. Will there be all facilities in a military camp? This is just that," Krishnaswamy said. He asked Nagesh Hegde: "Why did they excavate your Pooja room?"

"Sambajja has an eye on the jewellery in our family. He thought we may have buried it there." Gulvadimam looked at Nagesh Hegde in a way questioning about the jewellery.

"It is all Ambakka's department. She knows how to deal with such a situation," Nagesh Hegde whispered. When boys shout slogans and dogs start barking, she leaves the house taking clue. If they try to pass under a mat, we sneak below the *rangoli"* (A decoration drawn on the ground with coloured powder).

"Still, ask all to be careful. Do not keep money anywhere. Two years ago, at Kanagila in Ankola taluk, they had dug up the whole backyard of Bommayya Nayak. They may come again where there are still dues," Gulvadimam said.

As their lunch was getting over one young man came running. "He is from Bijjala, Shivamma's son. Manja, have you come from Vajgod?" Nagesh Hegde asked him.

"Yes. Confiscation is going on. Ganapayya and Seethakka had their cattle taken to far off Hulimakki Hillock. This was known to Manjayya. They sent Ugranis and brought all cattle to the spot. There were four bullocks, two cows and one buffalo. Saheb told him, 'Pay now at least, otherwise we will forfeit your cattle.' 'You can forfeit them, I will not pay,' said both Ganapayya and Seethakka. Now they are going to bring the confiscated cattle here to Sambajja's place."

"So they said they won't pay. That is nice. Where is the party now?"

"They are still there. They searched Seethakka's house and had secured four wooden planks. Nothing else was found. Then, search was going on in Ganapayya's house."

"Even after having confiscated so many heads of cattle, their dues are not adjusted?" Krishnaswamy asked.

"Ganapayya has to pay Rs.150. One pair of bullocks, one cow and a buffalo must be his. They evaluated them as worth Rs.100. In fact they do not assign even half the real price to any item. Seethakka has to pay Rs.60. A pair of bullocks and one cow will fetch at least Rs.70 or 75. They have also confiscated four planks, may be of jackfruit tree. Still they will say the price of cattle and planks has not reached rupees sixty. Was *Panchnama (Mahzar*) over, Manja?"

"A search was going on in Ganapayya's house. I came away."

"We go to Huliya now and congratulate him. Manja, will you go to Vajgod and get us the full report?" Gulvadimam said.

"Yes, I shall go to Vajagod, get full details and come to Huliya's house and we will meet you there."

"He anticipates your thoughts. He knows what you want him to do," Krishnaswamy said.

"Today the date is 27$^{th}$. Next two days these people will continue their arrogant acts. From March 3rd, all constables will be asked to assemble at Siddapur as we have our programme there on 4$^{th}$. Then these people have to stop their operations. Propaganda of our programme is extensive. As there are programmes in all taluks on the 4th, they have to manage here with the police from this taluk only. No outsiders can be brought. Then on the 11th we have announced Jungle Satyagraha in 18 centres in the taluk. Such programmes will check the intensity of the Japti programmes," Gulvadimam said.

As they were to come out, Paramayya's wife Shivamma and Parvati wanted Gulvadimam to go to their houses. "I have to go urgently. I have come to learn the details. I am happy you were bold in facing the situation. Now there is no time," said Gulvadimam.

"This guest from Sagar also joins you now?", Shivamma asked him.

"No, he had come to Gokarna. He is not connected with the movement. He will come with us for some distance. At night he will be here. I go to Itgi tonight."

Sambajja's family members were overhearing them. Nagesh Hegde came to know this, and he signalled to Gulvadimam not to talk. After covering some distance, Gulvadimam told Krishnaswamy. "You return to Nagesh Hegde's house. They are observing our movement and they want to know about you. Let them have no doubts now that you are connected with the movement." Cursing his bad luck, that he could not see Huliya, Krishnaswamy returned to Kelaginamane house.

□□

# Paeans to Freedom

Stand up you, hot-blooded young men
Set foot on the war field to fight for freedom.
Shining endurance is our sword
Rising confidence is our watchword
Hold the weapon of non-cooperation with valour
There is no hitting anybody in this war
Nor killing; it is a self-purificatory act.

A young man was singing this Kannada ballad loudly on a maidan. Even in the scorching sun, people had assembled. The number of the assembled was increasing minute by minute. People had come from the nooks and corners of Siddapur taluk. It was the celebration of Gandhi Day, at 4.00 p.m. At 1.00 p.m., the maidan was full. A young volunteer from Hubli, just 17, was singing the then popular ballad *Deshiya Dhumadhumme*. It was a highly inspiring song. The local people neither were accustomed to sing nor deliver speeches. They followed the instructions issued by the leaders. Krishnaswamy who was standing at a far off corner, felt like singing a song. He went near the platform and asked a person there whether he could also sing a song. "Oh yes, anybody can sing. We are searching for singers."

Krishnaswamy sang the famous song he had learnt at Bangalore. It was composed by the famous Kannada poet, B.M.Srikantayya. He stood up on the Chavadi. There was pin drop silence. He with his sweet but loud voice started singing.

When will you hold your head high O Bharatmata?
When will you show to the world your greatness?
Where are the great warriors
Peace and prosperity carriers?

He went on singing the long beautiful poem which was inspiring.
Oh. Bharatmata can't you hear our anguish?
How long are we in slavery to languish?
How long are we in slavery to languish?

The Assembly forgot to clap when the song was over, but they shed tears in real anguish. They sang in chorus the first two lines together with the singer loudly.

Next, there was a speech by Shiralagi Subraya Hegde.

"Brothers, lovers of freedom, as per the directions of Mahatma Gandhi, we have blown the war trumpet. We have picked up the *ranaveelya* (betel leaves to fulfil the oath). As it was decided at Gunjgod, people from the nooks and corners of Siddapur taluk have assembled here. The size of the assembly today and overwhelming enthusiasm of the participants have convinced us that we are going to win freedom soon. Now government has promulgated Section 144 banning procession and assembly of people. Still we shall go to taluk office in a procession. In our taluk till now 70 forfeitures have taken place. Thirty seven people have been arrested. Our Third Leader Gopal Shenoy has also been arrested. As our agitation is gathering momentum, our District Collector Clee is upset over the high-handedness of the officers here. It is rumoured that he may seek a transfer. It is all due to Mahatma Gandhi's blessings and the heroism and adventurous spirit of our own patriots like you, who have assembled here."

The speech was interrupted by slogans like 'Gandhi Sarkar Ku Jai' and 'Bharat Mata Ki Jai'.

"Today being the celebration of Gandhi Day, we hold a procession. As Section 144 is in vogue, the police may resort to *lathi* charge or even firing. But we should not prove to be cowards. We must surge like soldiers. We should follow non-violence. We should march forward as heroes. A step forward leads to heaven, a step backward takes us to hell. Nobody should be afraid of what all we have to face. Let us be heroes in the true sense of the term. Now the procession begins."

There was vigorous sloganeering. One person was singing a line and others repeated it in chorus as they marched:

"O heroes of Karnataka,
Here the sound of martial band
Utter the mantra of freedom
And take a firm stand"

The song was repeated.

Remove the slavery our darkness
Sun of freedom will arise,
The true heroism of Indians will appear
And our bitter enemy will disappear.

The procession proceeded with various patriotic songs in Kannada. Hundreds were marching. As the procession marched covering a furlong, the police numbering about 30, stopped them and resorted to *lathi* charge. But none left the spot. Some were attacked by bayonets and a few were wounded. Blood started oozing from the bodies. But the police force was too small to control the crowd. The processionists squatted on the road. The police arrested people in batches of 20 and took them to the station. Nobody thought of running away out of fear of arrest. They were firmly seated. About a 100 people were taken into custody, and the police did announce that the rest will not be arrested. They were asked to disperse. But people did not leave the spot.

There were warrants on Gulvadimam, Dodmane Nagesh Hegde and another worker called Akki Subbayya. They were sitting in a house in the town and were getting information about the procession. They came to know about the lathicharge. They also came to know that a prominent worker Madlegar Shantaramappa was knocked down and was severely beaten. Dodmane Ramanath Hegde had a bayonet wound on his neck and other processionists were treating him. All shops in the town were closed in protest against the lathicharge. People who were squatting were being served by the women and children in the town by providing them water, *shirabat*, etc. Somebody brought large bunches of plantain and distributed them. The police were threatening such sympathisers. But people were not deterred by such threats. Despite the police threatening, the people who were squatting (or on *dharana*) did not move. The police fired shots in the air. But nobody stirred. The Satyagrahis had been informed that they should squat till 8.00 p.m. It was getting dark. Singing and slogans continued. But there were some who thought in the darkness of the night the policemen may shoot and kill them. They whispered to each other.

By then three lady workers, Dodmane Mahadevamma, Dodmane Mahalakshmamma and Idakalgadde Manjamma reached the spot and surged forward amidst the squatted crowd. The police were non-plussed. They dared not stop them. The news that a constable had beaten a lady during *japti* at Bijjala had reached Collector Clee and he had expressed his dissatisfaction over the fact. After the procession of the 'Red Nuns' he had told the police to be careful in dealing with women. So the police did not try to check the three that came just then. Then they went round and greeted the assembly. After 8.00 p.m., the squatters dispersed shouting slogans loudly.

Those who had been arrested were severely beaten by the police and were asked to sign apology letters. 'You must sign apology letters before tomorrow morning, otherwise for having breached the 144 Section, you will be jailed for two years and a fine of thousand rupees will be imposed,' the police told them. Threats of various kinds were held out to terrorise them. They were neither provided drinking water nor food in the night. There was only petromax light and two lanterns. But none agreed to apologise. One Brahmin was taken to a lonely corner and threatened that his pigtail would be cut and his sacred thread would be torn. He agreed to apologise. Others were informed of this. Some felt that they may also apologise. In the morning, they were told that they have to apologise otherwise they will be punished. Some may be hanged was the threat held out. The police took down the names and addresses of all by calling them one by one.

The arrested ones had to sleep in the premises of the Police Station. Some did not sleep. There was no lock up in the Police Station to accommodate large number of people. What all had happened in the Station was made known to Gulvadimam and Dodmane Nagesh Hegde and they were very much worried. By 5 a.m., in batches of 15 or 20, the arrested persons were taken out for answering the nature's call. There was a well, a small water tank and some leaking tins.

Akki Subbayya went near the Station and mingled with the first batch of those who had come out. In their company he reached the Station in the dull light of the lamps. The Police could not know it.

"Has anybody agreed to apologise?" he asked some people. All people knew him as he was a prominent worker. They said 'no'. Having had to remain hungry in the night, the threat of the police had mellowed down at least some of them. "Nelamauu Keshav Bhatta has agreed to apologise," somebody told him. Akki Subbayya knew Keshav Bhatta well. He located him in the group.

"Keshavanna you are going to apologise? If you do it, what will Padmatte (Mrs.Keshav Bhatta) say? She will come and undertake a fast in front of the jail and will go to jail. Yesterday Dodmane Mahadevamma and other ladies had come. You saw them in the evening. They are by now reaching the houses of each and every arrested person. Women from the houses of the arrested will come here in an hour. By seven o' clock there will be an assembly of women here."

"No Maaraya, I am not apologising," Keshava Bhatta told him.

"Somebody told me you were the first to agree to apologise?"

"Who told you? No, I am sure not to."

"You are not offering an apology – well and good. People unnecessarily make false allegations. Women from the houses of those who apologise will come here, undertake Satyagraha and go to jail," Akki Subbayya announced somewhat loudly. "Dodmane Mahadevamma, Kallala Kaveramma, Idakalagadde Manjamma who were all here yesterday, have gone to your villages and sent messages to fetch your ladies to go to jail. You may apologise, go home, take care of your cattle, do the cooking and take care of your children…. When you men apologise, how will the women bear with the idea? You have seen the furious widows holding procession the other day?"

Seeing Shavemane Narayana Shastry, Subbayya told him: "Your wife Seetakka has come yesterday night and has stayed in Chandraghatgi's house. She was telling that 'If my husband tenders apology, I'll undertake Satyagraha'."

Well-known henpecked Shastri told Subbayya: "No Maharaya. I am not apologising. I will go to jail. Please go and tell her."

"Now Seethakka will come here to speak to you. Somebody told her you are likely to apologise."

"I am inside here. How can I tell her? All the women will court arrest and will come here," Subbayya said.

"Hear me Subbayya, ask her not to come here. I am not seeking apology. Please tell her."

"How can I tell her? I am here inside. All women will get arrested and come here. Yesterday itself Dodamane Mahadevi and others had visited the place."

The rumour that there would be a procession of women, and they would court arrest spread all over the jail. 'Go home, take care of your cattle and do the cooking and take care of your children,' these words of Subbayya resounded in the ears of the arrested and hit the nail on the head. That women's procession will arrive caused extreme reaction. As some women had come the previous night, police stopped firing also.

"No, I am not apologising. Come what may," one of them said. "I too. Let them hang us," another person said. "Don't mind even if I am sent to the Andamans, I shall not apologise," was another reaction.

It was 8.00 a.m. We should be provided with breakfast, was the chorus of the arrested.

"You had promised to apologise and go. Why do you want breakfast now?" one Jamadar said.

"No, I am not apologising…. I shall stay as government guest.

Provide us breakfast," he replied.

All shouted that they will not apologise. Around the Police Station, town people assembled. It was not possible for the police to attack people with weapons as they did in the night. The Sub-Inspector came to know of this. He sent for Nelemavu Keshava Bhatta.

"Fauzdar Saheb, I am prepared to go to the gallows. Send me to the Andamans. I am not apologising. You have cut my sacred thread. I will report the matter to the Collector sahab."

"You stay in jail and eat food cooked by the untouchables?"

"What is the alternative? I do not mind. This is for Independence of the country."

"Offer a *jaamin* (surety) and you get released."

"My land is rented one. I can't offer *jaamin.* If you want to confiscate my land, it is not mine."

"I am not asking your *jaamin*-land. Offer us a *jaamin*."

"What *jaamin*? I do not have anything of that kind with me. If you want hang me."

The Sub-Inspector found it difficult to face the new situation. He sent for other 2 to 3 people and got the same reply. He heard the rumour that a procession of women was going to come. If all these people were to be detained here, how to arrange for their food? There was no space to detain so many people in the lock-up. They will have to be taken to Karwar Jail. 'If the Collector comes to know that I have arrested so many people, he will be furious. He has an impression that we are behaving in a high-handed way. It is rumoured that the Collector wants a transfer or he will resign as he is unable to regulate his subordinates.' That was the trend of the Sub Inspector's thought.

After detaining some 6 or 7 people, he released all. They shouted slogans and lead a procession. The released were asked by Akki Subbayya to go to Puttayyanakere (tank) in the town where Dodmane Nagesh Hegde had sent a cart load full of ripe jackfruits and mangoes.

Among those detained and charge sheeted, Kelaginamane Ramakrishna Hegde was one, who was later sentenced to three months' imprisonment.

□□

# Satyagrahi Buffalo!

Various items forfeited from different places in the taluk were to be taken to Siddapur Taluk Office. As Krishnaswamy was asked to stay at Lambapura centre, he went to Lambapur the next day of the procession at Siddapur. Premananda Kalyanpur, originally from Mangalore, had come from Bombay to work with him at Lambapur. Earlier he had worked at Siddapur for some days. He had a melodious voice and was very courteous in behaviour. But they were not staying in a single place. Almost everyday they changed their residence. They could go to any village around and stay with anybody. Participants in No-Tax movement or not, all the hosts were sympathetic to the movement and were co-operative. Some invited them for breakfast and some for lunch or dinner. Even the uneducated joined them to walk miles together, to show them the way to unknown places. Those who considered them as Brahmins, instead of offering cooked food, offered them plantains or tender coconut. As their names had not been entered in police records, they had no difficulty in going round and speaking to the people about the movement. They knew the supporters of the movement in every village or hamlet. Krishnaswamy had secured a map of the taluk.

The items forfeited in Kelaginamane and from Vajagodu and Danamavu had been stored in the house of Kelaginamane Sambajja. One Jamadar with a few police constables and some 7 to 8 Ugranis came to collect the items. Two bullock carts were also commissioned.

One was from Sambajja and another from Lambapur Patel. Nobody else was willing to lend his cart. Though Vajagod Manjayya had agreed to lend his cart, somebody had removed the pins of the axle of the cart (*kadanis*). The cart could not be moved without the *kadanis*.

As the vessels were in good number, they could not be easily accommodated in a single cart. Still they arranged it in a single cart, and the cart looked like a tall decorated temple car.

Taking the cattle was a difficult task. As they were tied and confined to a single place for five or six days and not sufficiently fed, they were feeling uneasy. The moment the knot tied to the post or peg was loosened, some of the cattle ran away. Vajagodu Ganapayya's bullocks ran straight to Vajagodu.

The Ugranis running in pursuit of them was a kind of entertainment to the Monkey Brigade. They shouted and indulged in sloganeering. One buffalo after moving a distance of 100 feet squatted refusing to rise. The 'lathi charge' by the police could not make it budge. "O polisappa, you do lathi charge on the buffalo?" one boy asked. The constable stared at the boy in anger with his eyes widened. "Now I will be reduced to ashes as polisappa has released fire from his eyes", the boy joked. As the constables hit the buffalo continuously the boys sang in chorus: "M*ahishasura mardana namami, Mahishasura mardana*" (O, killer of Mahishasura, I salute thee). Four persons held the four legs of the buffalo and tried to put the buffalo on its feet. They twisted its tail, to no avail. 'It may get up on its own, and then you bring it to Siddapur', they instructed the Ugrani. The rest of the cattle party moved to the main road. After that, two Ugranis came back from the road to go to Vajagod to fetch the bullocks from Vajagod. One boy threw from a long distance the cart breaks (*kadanis*) at the Ugranis and shouted: "These belong to Vajagod Manjayya's cart. Return them to him", and they ran away fast.

When their vessels were loaded on the cart, Paramayya's wife Shivamma and daughter Rukku began to weep. Women in Nagesh Hegde's house also wept. They were highly attached to the vessels, and more than that the cattle. They had brought up these cows with love. They were like members of the family. Shivamma was hoping against hope, as the vessels were in the house of Sambajja, perhaps by some Godly act they might be returned. But her hope was belied.

Krishnaswamy and Premanand who just arrived after the party left, also had their eyes filled with tears.

All men had not come out of the house. But women were standing in a group outside. Krishnaswamy went near them. He was not sure what to talk. The women stopped shedding tears. Silence was more powerful than words. Expression on the face of the ladies spoke 'your being with us here itself is our solace'.

A girl loudly said, "Krishnabhava has come." Paramayya came out and invited him in. By then Nagesh Hegde and Subraya also reached the place.

"I shall give you *asare* (something to drink)," Shivamma said and invited them in her house. They went in.

"You were not to be seen since morning. Yesterday, also you did not come?" said Paramayya. Nagesh Hegde also asked the same question.

"Yesterday we had visited Kyadagi, Itagi, Kasge and Sampakhand to meet people. Forest Satyagraha will be launched on the 11th you know? At Lambapura we are holding Satyagraha with your brother Narayana as the leader. You got the news?"

"What is it?"

"Now I came to know at Siddapura six people were held on the 5th morning. All of them were punished to undergo three months' term and a fine of Rs.50."

"We heard this news today in the noon. Our Ramakrishna also is convicted. They had sent a word yesterday night. The volunteer who came here from Siddapur did not find the right way. He loitered in the jungle and reached here at twelve noon. In the morning he reached the stream. He saw the police standing there. Some of the constables were known to him. So to escape their attention, he waited there. They were busy arranging the carts and loading them. Somehow he reached here at twelve o'clock. He had his lunch here, and left via Bijjala. Tomorrow they may come here to collect the fine imposed on Ramakrishna. Chandraghatgi had sent a word with the boy," Nagesh

Hegde told him.

"I wanted to warn you about the same thing. Now we will leave. It is dangerous to be here for long," Krishnaswamy said.

"No, don't worry. Just now the police have left. They have to transport all seized goods to Siddapur."

"The Kite-Eye has gone with the cart. If he returns, our boys will inform us", said Subraya.

"Then he does not know that we are here?" asked Premanand.

"No. They were busy trying to make the squatted buffalo get up. What happened later Subraya?" Paramayya asked.

"After they left, the Ugrani went to answer the call of nature. Then the buffalo got up and ran in the direction of Vajagod."

"What did Ugrani do?"

"What can he do? How much can he run? The buffalo ran towards the forest. There is no trace of it. They say buffaloes are mentally less equipped. But this buffalo is really intelligent. Waiting for Ugrani to go it ran away, ending its *dharana.* It seems to know about the Satyagraha!" All laughed aloud.

"Last time Ganapayya's bullocks which were forfeited and taken to Lambapur escaped after two days and returned to Vajagod. This year this buffalo has escaped. This buffalo also belongs to him. What kind of training he might have given to them? God knows."

"Just as Seva Dal holds camps and trains volunteers, the cattle likely to be confiscated by the government also must be trained in camps and Vajagodu Ganapayya should be their Captain," said Subraya. All laughed.

"Krishna Bhat, the song you sang at Siddapur the other day was first class. Really top class," said Paramayya. While he said this, Krishnaswamy could see Rukku's face brightening.

"Yes. It was said to be really good, Subraya told me. What song is that?" asked Shivamma. In the meanwhile beaten rice *happala* and *kashaya* were served to all.

"What song? In a destroyed village the survivor has to be treated as Patel. At a place where there is nobody to sing, a donkey is the class one singer," said Krishnaswamy, jocularly.

"Today you two take your supper in our house," Paramayya invited the visitors.

"How are we to stay at a place where dangerous Kite-Eye lives?" Krishnaswamy expressed his concern.

"Do not worry. The talk in our house, they can overhear. But not from this house," Nagesh Hegde said.

"Why had Dodmane Ramnath Hegde come to you?" Paramayya asked Nagesh Hegde.

"Oh, he caused anxious moments to me. Ramnath had been arrested together with our Ramakrishna the other day."

"He had been seriously wounded with a bayonet. How is he now?" Paramayya asked him.

"Here at Siddapur he was bandaged and administered some medicine. Next day he was taken to Karwar jail. There he was treated in the Civil Hospital. To the left of his neck there is a small wound. The sharp edge of the bayonet had pierced that part. A vein must have been cut. The flow of blood was horrifying. But there is no danger. Anyway, for the first time, blood was shed in the taluk."

"But why did he come? Is he released?"

"Yes, he is released. We are four brothers and anyone among us will not go to jail but stay behind. Someone must take care of the family. That was Ramnath's request. He wants to undertake Jungle Satyagraha and court arrest. If I say yes, he will court arrest", he said.

"Why should you say yes?"

"He wants me to shoulder the responsibility. Quite a critical situation."

"What responsibility?", Paramayya asked.

"It is a severe headache," said Nagesh Hegde.

As Nagesh Hegde did not wish to tell anything more, others stopped their queries.

"In our area Kyadgi, Itgi and Lambapur are the three centres where we have planned Jungle Satyagraha. At Kyadgi, Ramanath Hegde, at Lambapur your brother Naryana Hegde and at Itgi Namdhari Timma will lead the Satyagraha. At every centre at least 20 people should join. That is our aim. And at every centre, there has to be some women. At Kyadgi, 3 to 4 ladies are ready. At Lambapur and Itgi, no women have been forth coming. Women with small children find it difficult to go to jail. Where will they leave the kids when they are arrested?" Krishnaswamy said.

"Last time no woman was arrested. But who knows? This year they may arrest women too. In our house my wife is carrying. Ramakrishna's wife went to Hoskoppa, her father's house. Narayana's son is four year old. Subraya has been married only four months ago," said Nagesh Hegde.

"All right, I will send my wife," said Subraya.

"No no, she is just married girl. 'Have we sent our girl to your house to send her to jail?' her parents may ask. No. Do not send her. I will ask Narayana's wife to go. Call her," Nagesh Hegde said. Rukku ran to call her.

"I don't have to ask my father-in-law. Let her go," said Subraya.

"No, no. She is just married. If Narayana Hedge's wife agrees, let her be sent." By then, Nagesh Hegde's younger sister Gangatte, elder sister Ambakka and Subraya's wife came there. Rukku had already apprised them of the issue being discussed.

"All the three of us are prepared to join Jungle Satyagraha," Gangatte announced.

"Shabbas," said Krishnaswamy. He congratulated them.

"I am also happy," said Premanand.

"Ambakka, you please don't go. Now your responsibility has doubled," said Nagesh Hegde.

"Yes, Ambe, there is already one responsibility on you. You don't join us. I and Lakshmi will go. Not you," said Gangatte.

Krishnaswamy, thinking that there may be a serious responsibility on Ambakka, said: "Two are more than enough."

"Appa, with Gangatte I too will go for Satyagraha," Rukku said.

"You too want to go? Is it like going for a lunch?," Paramayya objected. Rukku's face grew pale.

"In case she wants to join allow her. Anyway elderly Gangatte is there," said Krishnaswamy.

"Suppose she is arrested, what should we do? She is still unmarried you see," Paramayya interrupted.

"I will go to Satyagraha, not Rukku," said Shivamma. "If I am arrested Rukku will take care of the home."

"What! You want to go, leaving the unmarried girl at home?" Paramayya objected.

"Paramayya, you your wife and daughter can join the Satyagraha, I will take care of your children, Shankara and Saraswati in our house," Nagesh Hegde suggested.

"I will take care of the children if they go," reassured Ambakka.

Three persons from a single house, father, mother and daughter participating in the movement will be big news. Please think over it Paramayya Hegde," said Krishnaswamy.

Because her husband had gone to jail, her daughter's marriage had been held up, was Shivamma's complaint earlier. But now her offer to join the movement was a matter of great surprise to Krishnaswamy. He felt that the sanctity of this National Sacrifice (*yajnya*) was magnetic. It was attracting more and more people to the altar of self-sacrifice.

"Please think it over Paramayya. There are still four more days. No hurry," said Krishnaswamy.

"From our house Narayana, his wife and Gangatte are going. Today or tomorrow the police will also drag me on the charge of sedition for having not paid the Land Tax. Let Subraya alone be in our house to take care of the household. Please think and decide," said Narayana Hegde.

That night Krishanswamy and Premanand took food in Paramayya's house. Krishanswamy had missed such wholesome meal for many days. Rukku was running around like a young deer and serving food. Shivamma told him again that night that all the three of them will join the Satyagraha. In case they are jailed, he should come to Kelaginamane often and enquire about their children. At the same time, she said that members of Nagesh Hegde's family were good people and she had little to worry.

"In case I am arrested, what shall I do?" joked Krishnaswamy.

"Minors, I was told, are not arrested. Is it true? In case Rukku is not arrested, she will be back here. Ambakka takes care of her. But you too please keep an eye on her," said Shivamma.

"How old is she?" Premanand asked.

"She has grown tall like a banana plant. She completed only 14 last Phalguna month. The girl has grown up and we have not married her is the criticism we face. Twice my husband went to jail. So her marriage could not be held. If we attain Swaraj this year, and there is an end to my husband's jail visits, I hope her marriage will take place this year. Let the third jail visit be the last one. They say calamities visit only three times: *Murakke muktaya*," said Shivamma.

The innocence of Shivamma made Krishnaswamy smile. He pitied her ignorance about the route of Swaraj which is miles and miles long.

Subraya, with the help of a dry coconut leaf torch, guided them till Lambapur in the night.

Rukku had several dreams of the movement during the night. How should she act during the agitation? Krishnaswamy was guiding her. In her dream she felt that he held her hand and pressed it and told her to be bold. In her dream, she had gone to jail. Swaraj had come! And she and Krishnaswamy got......

□□

# Cowed Down

The Siddapur Tahshildar's compound and the taluk office had given shelter to scores of forfeited cattle. The taluk office surroundings were full of heaps of cowdung, ponds of cows urine, unbearable stench and swarms of mosquitoes. One or two calves had died of indigestion or starvation. When the scavengers were sent for to take away the carcasses, they refused to touch the carcasses of calves that had been forfeited from freedom fighters; even if they were to go hungry, they did not want to partake the beef of confiscated animals.

The Sub-Inspector ordered that after milking, the milk must be sent to his house. The constables who tried to milk them were greeted by kicks of the cattle. The calves partook all the milk available, suffered indigestion and eased themselves with watery dung.

As per order, the cattle were to be auctioned as early as possible. March 9$^{th}$ was fixed as the date of auction. On that day hundreds of men and women surrounded the office and engaged in picketing. There was lathi charge and more than 40 people were arrested. In the evening five were detained and the rest were released. As nobody came forward to bid, the professional butchers were invited from Hubli.

In the meanwhile, Jungle Satyagraha was organised in 18 places in the taluk, and everywhere there were 15 to 20 Satyagrahis and in certain places the participants were 100. After informing the Forest Department of the Satyagraha in advance, cutting only twigs from the trees was the way of protest. Only 30 persons were arrested and brought to Siddapur. These included Kelaginamane Narayana Hegde and Paramayya.

On March 15th butchers came from Hubli. A bus load of police came from Karwar. The public was not permitted to go beyond 100 feet from the taluk office. *Bandobast* was strong. Eight to ten butchers from Hubli were present. If the auction succeeded, the morale of the participants in Satyagraha was likely to sink. Dodamane Narayana Hegde, Gulvadimam and others discussed the issue. Premanada Kalyanpur offered to take risk to stop the auction. In case his effort did not succeed, hundreds should rush and surround the taluk office, braving lathis and bullets, was the decision.

But on the day of auction, Imamsab, a Congress worker of Sirsi joined the butchers' company that night and reached the Taluk office. He said to the butchers that he had come from Malgi, a nearby town. As the moment of auction approached he started talking in Urdu. "Brothers, this Hindustan of ours is great in the whole world (*Sare Jahnase Accha*). Hindustan is ruled by the Kafir British. A *jehad* is going on to drive them out. These are the cattle of *gazis* who are participants in the *jehad.* Killing them is a great sin. Khan Abdul Ghaffar Khan, the leader of the Khuda-I-Khidmatgars is in the jail of *harami* British. Many Khuda-I-Khidmatgars have been killed by the British police. You will be cursed by such *shahids* (martyrs). Butcher me before cutting these cows." The police caught hold of him and took him away. He kept on speaking even while being dragged away.

The Talshildar was determined to continue the auction. Some seven or eight cows were brought forward.

Neatly dressed Premanand Kalyanpur, holding a thick file in his hand and posing like a government servant silently crossed the police cordon and came to the office premises.

"Brothers," he said in a sweet voice and tried to address the assembled. "I am a college student from Bombay. I have come here to participate in the great *yajnya* (sacrifice) being held under the guidance of Mahatma Gandhi. Protection of cows is one of the programmes of the Mahatma. I was highly pained to know that cows are auctioned here to the butchers. I am very much upset."

The talk of Premanand in an appealing tone created commotion in the minds of the butchers. Those who were examining cows were mentally disturbed. They left the spot and slowly moved away. The officer conducting the auction got confused and frightened. It was a peculiar situation. "Please stop your lecture. Auctioning is cancelled," he announced. Vociferous slogan shouting by hundreds from a distance was heard.

"Let God Gopalakrishna bless you, for this act of merit" Premanand said loudly with folded hands. The officer lifted his files and went in.

"Brothers, do not participate in these sinful acts. Fifteen days ago they forfeited a milch cow from Bilgi. An eight month old child nourished by the cow was starved of milk and died. Who is answerable to this sinful event? If you butcher cows what happens to the children nourished by them? Why should milch cows be cut to pieces? Don't you have children?" While saying all this, Premanand was arrested. Those who had come to participate in the auction disappeared.

The Officer who had come to conduct the auction told the Tahshildar that he could not conduct the auction and that the Collector had told him not to conduct the auction if peace was likely to be disturbed. The Tahshildar ordered the release of all cattle. The auction had been cancelled. The news spread all around. Many Satyagrahis whose cattle had been forfeited returned their receipts to the office and took their cattle back. Many women of Siddapur garlanded the released cows, put vermilion mark on their forehead, performed the ceremony waving the lamp (*aarati*) and gave a send off to the cows brought from far off villages.

"This is a major victory for Satyagraha. The Pandavas got the cows released after *gograhana* (theft of cows) at Viratanagari. Now the final victory at Kurukshetra is assured," wrote the Satyagraha Bulletin, referring to the Mahabharata episode.

Except the cattle that were regularly milked, the remaining were to be sent to places away from the houses, to even neighbouring villages or taluks like Honnavar, Kumta, Sirsi etc. For the convenience of the villagers *goshalas* (shelter for animals) were planned to be started at places like Harishi and Keladi in Shimoga district. This was the decision of the Congress.

The bullocks forfeited from Kelaginamane Nagesh Hegde's house were returned. The next day came the news that jewels worn by Ramakrishna Hegde's wife who had gone to Hoskoppa to her parents house were forfeited by the police by issuing a warrant. Chungadi Sambajja himself had accompanied the officials to the place. In fact jewellery is woman's property (*streedhana*) and confiscating wife's property for husband's dues to the government is illegal. But this illegal activity continued unquestioned.

"Why don't we shatter Sambajja's limbs?" Subraya asked Krishnaswamy.

"Please do not do it. This is absolutely against Gandhiji's path of non-violence. Please, please do not think in terms of violence. Bear with all inconveniences," Krishnaswamy told him. "In case we indulge in violence, the British may bring the army, use guns and shoot us down. The movement will be over. This has happened in many places due to over-enthusiastic workers, not trained in non-violence. Because of the Chauri-Chaura violence, Gandhiji withdrew the movement in 1922. In case they hit us on the left cheek, we shall show the right cheek. This helps us in gaining public sympathy. What happened at Jalianwala? The violence by the British created wide commotion. Men like Motilal Nehru joined the movement because of that."

*Japti* progressed with great momentum. Small pox was widespread in the district. Taluk Leader Dodmane Nagesh Hegde did not even visit his house and was underground. A warrant had been issued for his arrest. They came to his house to collect revenue dues. He was not at home. They confiscated his wife's jewellery. Several necklaces, bangles, her golden girdle and a bracelet (*vanki)* were confiscated. While preparing *mahzar*, they recorded the bracelet as *onkibale* (bracelet bangle). Later it was clandestinely changed as *onkebale* (the ring of a pounding instrument) and replaced the golden bracelet by an iron ring. An officer pocketed the golden bracelet. Wherever there was scope the officials filled their pockets with jewels by recording confiscated goods falsely.

Knowing the falsehood perpetrated by the government officials

Dodmane Nagesh Hegde did nothing. Success of the movement was his main aim. His wife suffered from small pox. The police were waiting to see when he would come home to see her. He never turned up. Finally the lady breathed her last. The police waited to see whether he would come to see her. But he did not turn up even for her final rites. The final rites were performed in his absence. The story of sacrifice of this rich man of the taluk was a great source of inspiration to the No-Tax Payers and freedom fighters.

When the final rites of the lady were being performed, at the Neralmane camp Gulvadimam and other workers faced a serious problem. Herur and neighbouring villages had been surrounded by a bus load of police coming from Karwar since 5.00 in the morning. Nobody could enter the surrounded villages nor could anybody come out. Some leaders of the movement had taken shelter in those villages. That was the reason why police had encircled these villages. Police went to every house in the village and tortured the people. If this problem is not solved people may feel that every village will have to face similar situation, and their morale may evaporate.

Krishnaswamy, Pundlik Shenoy and Gulvadimam were equally worried. A few days back, Umesh a worker from Bombay, had joined them. All of them walked and reached Sagar in the night. With the help of local Congressmen, Bapat and others, they got a bulletin cyclostyled in red ink. For Umesh, who was tall, well-built and fair looking they got a red military dress stitched overnight. He twisted his moustache like military men by applying oil. His bedding roll was given to him. He took the bundle of red bulletins. Next day at 9 in the morning he boarded the Sagar-Sirsi bus. Everybody in the bus was staring at him. When the bus reached Mysore State boarder, the bus was stopped and a policeman came to check whether any khadi-clad person connected with the movement was there. The constable came near Umesh and he stared at the constable with wide eyes. The constable was frightened. To which place this guy was going, the constable secretly asked the conductor. 'To Siddapur', the conductor whispered. The bus was allowed to proceed. As the bus moved about ten yards, Umesh threw down 3-4 bulletins he had. The constable picked them. The bus moved on.

When the bulletin fell into the hands of the Sagar police, they were highly upset. "Red Shirts from North West Frontier to Canara" was the heading. "To protect the people of Canara from the high-handedness and atrocities of the police hundreds of Red Shirts are likely to visit Canara," the Bulletin read.

Immediately two constables were sent to Talaguppa and they sent a telegram to Siddapur Police Station: "**SIRSI-SAGAR BUS NOW ARRIVING HAS REDSHIRT ˇ MEET AT BUS STAND**."

There was a Jamadar and three constables in the police station at Siddapur. The Jamadar ordered one constable: "Go to the bus stand – in Sagar Sirsi bus. Redshirt is coming." He himself could not understand what was the matter. The constable dared not seek the details from the Jamadar.

By the time he could reach the bus stand, the scheduled bus had already reached. Umesh got down and distributed a few bulletins to bystanders. To small group assembled there he shouted "Red Shirt, Red Shirt, Kempangi". Seeing the constable, he called him in Hindi "Idhar Aao" (come here). Constable saluted Umesh. He handed over the bedroll to the constable. He asked him to guide him to the police station. (*Chalo police station ko*, in Hindi). He distributed the bulletin on the way. "Red shirts are coming to help the freedom fighters," the Bulletin said. The rumour of arrival of Red Shirts spread. The Jamadar came out, saluted Umesh, thinking he must be somebody important. Umesh entered the Station. The Sub-Inspector's chair was empty. He occupied it.

"Where is the Sub-Inspector," he asked the Jamadar.

"He has gone out, Sir."

"Call him," Umesh said in Hindi.

"He has gone far away, Sir."

"Call him. Thousands of Red Shirts are expected. Tell him, go immediately."

By then, townsmen, mostly Muslims surrounded the Station premises. Taluk Magistrate was also not available.

Jamadar sent a constable with a bunch of bulletins on a cycle to

Herur. He speeded and reached Herur. He met the sub-inspector and handed over the pamphlet. "Red Shirt has come and is in the station," he told him. Thousands of Red Shirts were arriving was the impression created. He gathered considerable number of constables. A passenger bus passing by was stopped and all the passengers were made to alight. While passengers were abusing, he filled the bus with constables. The bus came to Siddapur Police Station.

Villagers of Herur and nearby villages who were being harassed by the police were saved.

Here at Siddapur, Umesh standing on the station's compound wall started lecturing in Kannada: "Don't be afraid, Don't pay tax. Don't be afraid to participate in Civil Disobedience. Lakhs of Red Shirts support you."

The sub-inspector and other constables with guns approached him. "Sub-Inspector, I am alone, I have no arms. Don't shoot. Don't be afraid," Umesh said in Kannada lifting his hands.

After all he was alone, unarmed, said the sub-inspector after heaving a sigh of relief and asked him to jump down from the compound wall. People clapped wildly. Umesh was arrested.

Relieving the villagers of Herur from the atrocities they were facing with the help of one Red Shirt became a big news in the district. Morale of the freedom fighters was at its height. Umesh was sentenced to three years jail for having distributed seditious literature.

Three days after this event government publicised that confiscated goods will be auctioned. As the bulletins had announced that none should be bidders, the auctioning was boycotted. There was rumour that about one-thousand Namdharis would come in a procession to the taluk office from Bedkani.

The doors of taluk office were closed. Some Ugranis, Patels who had come, and some petty government officials and constables present there persuaded the people to buy the auctioned goods. Something worth one rupee was auctioned for four annas. A copper pitcher worth four rupees was auctioned for one rupee. Still, the total receipt from auction hardly exceeded three hundred rupees. Some 70-80 sackful of vessels still remained unsold.

In the third week of March, Ghanekar and Karmarkar who were leading the movement in Ankola taluk were arrested. Krishnaswamy and two others were sent to Ankola taluk by District Congress Committee President Chandraghatgi. By then Venkatramayya had come to guide the movement in Siddapur which he had guided in 1930. He stayed at Tadagalale in Sagar taluk, very near the border of Siddapur taluk and guided and directed the movement. He had persuaded Patels in Sirsi taluk to resign *en masse* in 1930 and was already famous. His wife Gauramma worked with him. As Uttara Kannada (Canara) was in Bombay Presidency and Sagar taluk was in princely Mysore State, the Police from Siddapur could not enter Sagar to arrest anybody easily.

Krishnaswamy went to Gokarna with the help of a guide. By foot he reached a village called Sagadageri and stayed in the house of Biranna Nayak, a peasant of the Nadavar caste. He was in the forefront of the movement in the taluk.

□□

# Women Save the Day

The Nadavars who had fought for
Vijayanagara Kingdom
And enjoyed the feast of freedom
Are grieved to see Bharatmata in shackles.
Now they are ready to fight for freedom.
They dare to face the British, by preparing salt,
And they do not want to pay salt tax.
Those who fight for the country are real countrymen.
All the Nadavars respond to the call of Gandhiji.
We have a brave heart. And we will fight.

This chorus song in Kannada sung by young boys and girls awoke Krishnaswamy from his morning slumber at Sagadageri. It was the song chanted by the young ones who were holding the Prabhat Pheri (morning procession). A group of 30 to 40 urchins, holding the tricolour flag were moving in the narrow streets of the village. When Krishnaswamy finished his morning ablutions, he was offered a yellow liquid *hombesaru*, made of green gram which he had never tasted. Its odour was somewhat pungent, but its taste was delicious. Biranna Nayak was told that Ankola Taluk Leader Rama Nayak had arrived.

Basagod Rama Nayak, the stormy petrel, came in, and after greeting Krishnaswamy, told him, "We shall immediately start to our

Koorve camp. Take your bag and baggage."

Biranna Nayak introduced Rama Nayak to Krishnaswamy. "He is our Taluk Leader, Basagod Rama Nayak," Biranna Nayak told the new comer. "Ramanna, you are always in a hurry. Have a tumbler of *hombesaru*."

"No, I have no time. I have to send two other persons who came with me elsewhere. I have to take Krishna Bhatta to Koorve. If it is late, police patrol will start."

Krishnaswamy stood up with his bag and baggage. As they came out, bidding goodbye to Biranna Nayak, two boys took the baggage from his hands and walked with them. The Gangavali river was reflecting golden lustre in the morning sun. The tall coconut palms on either banks were reflecting in the river water. Small boats were moving here and there disturbing the reflections. Some persons were throwing their nets wide to catch fish. Some langoti wearing boys standing in knee-deep water, were collecting fish shells. Some people wearing langoti were there covering their head with small turbans.

"You too will have to wear similar dress here. If you wrap yourself in *panche* police will identify you and arrest you. You will have to wear *langoti*," Rama Nayak instructed Krishnaswamy. The instruction was in the tone of an order of the 'Dictator'. "Next we will reach the village Joog. It was here that Karmarkar was arrested. All these villages are our forts. The Nadavars here have completely resorted to No-Tax. We have 40 villages here. Only at Uluvare there are Halakki Vokkals. They too have not paid revenue. More than hundred forfeitures have taken place. Vessels of copper, bronze and brass, cots, cupboards, jewellery, buffaloes and cows have been forfeited. Confiscation is continuing. Now we are going to Koorve. Look over there that island in the river. The place is called Koorve, and *koorve* literary means an island."

There was a patch of land in the middle of the river, full of coconut palms.

"Is there river beyond the place?" Krishnaswamy queried.

"Yes, the same river has branched to create an island. Here is our camp. The police can't reach the place easily. If they come from the left bank we can escape from the right. There are boys to watch for Police. Till the peak of the rainy season we can stay here. With heavy rains, this place gets submerged and a few people living here go elsewhere. This is just two miles away from the sea shore."

They entered the riverbed, and after wading through water a few steps, they got into a small boat. Rama Nayak told the boatman, "This is a new volunteer. He will be here. This is Vasu, the boatman. On the other bank there is Timma, his younger brother oaring the boat," Rama Nayak told Krishanswamy. They crossed the river in 7 to 8 minutes. "You please put on your footwear. This area is full of fish shells. They hurt your feet," Rama Nayak said. At the lowest level there in the riverbed were fish shells. They reached the bank wading through the river. The two boys ran forward with the baggage they had. Two men came to welcome Krishnaswamy with smile on their lips.

"This is Mathanda from Coorg. This is Anatarao Chikodi from Belgaum. Where has Devayya gone?" asked Rama Nayak.

"He has gone to the well to take bath," said Anantrao in his slang Belgaum Kannada and held the hand of Krishnaswamy. At a distance of 100 yards, there were three thatched huts. "This is our camp, bow your head and come in," said Rama Nayak and took them all in.

Even inside, the roof was very low. Outside, in the corridor, the baskets and nets were stocked clearly indicating that it was the house of a fisherman. Twenty steps away to the right and left there were two more huts. In each house there were two women and children who were looking at the new comer with curious eyes. Not far away was a well, but it had no pulley and water had to be lifted by throwing down a pot with a rope. The river water was salty due to the nearness of the sea. Krishanswamy was invited to sit on a grass mat. "Anantrao, you tell him all the work he has to undertake. I will go now…. Ram Mahale has brought paper, stencil sheet and ink from Karwar Collector's office. Those things will reach Krishna Nayak's house at Hichkad. You Santu and Narayana must go and fetch the items here in the night," Rama Nayak told the boys.

"Now, how are we to celebrate the National Week? Have the

instructions reached all villages, Rama Nayak?" Anantrao asked. "We have all the instruction in the bulletin. Why are you worried? Those who cannot read also know them. The bulletin will be read out. From April 6th, there has to be flag hoisting daily and *prabhat* pheri. Also *pheri* in the evenings everywhere. And Jungle Satyagraha will be held everyday in some places. On 13th, there will be a procession at Ankola. Everybody is informed. Today I am going to Basagod, Surve and Pojgeri. Preparations have to be made at these places for Jungle Satyagraha. At Basgod, my mother will lead Jungle Satyagraha. At Mogata, Shirugunji and Talagadde Venkatramana Nayak has been assigned the responsibility. Babu Nayak has gone to Gundbala and Hillur. In all the surrounding villages propaganda is on. In seven days, Jungle Satyagraha is arranged in 12 places."

"How many women are joining?"

"Everywhere women are joining. In Basagod my mother, and at Kanagila Bommakka will lead. In three other places, women are sure to participate."

"But Bommakka's husband is in jail," Anantrao said.

"What does it matter? She said that she will leave her children at her sister's house. She is prepared to go to jail. Day after tomorrow, there is auctioning of liquor shops at Karwar and she is willing to join picketing against the auction at Karwar. Last year by picketing we had succeeded in closing all the liquor shops in Ankola and Kumta taluks as we did not allow auctioning. We will do that again. From Hichkad, Bole, Vandige and Kanagila fifty women are ready to join this time for picketing. Honnavar Martu Naik has said that he will send a bus on that day at four o'clock in the morning. From Karwar town too some women will join, Krishnarao Haldipurkar said."

"Where did you meet Krishana Rao?"

"He had come to Ankola yesterday to Bab Kamat's house. I too had been there."

"Any letter from Subrao, his brother?"

"Yes, He has recovered. Bettegowda also has recovered. He will come after eight days."

"Where is Bettegowda now?", Krishnaswamy enquired.

Bettegowda was a Seva Dal volunteer from Hassan district. During Salt Satyagraha he had come to Ankola.

"You know him? He was suffering from jaundice. It was difficult for him to follow necessary diet and other conditions . For first eight days he was in Hari Pai's house at Ankola. Then we sent him on a steamer to Goa, to Subbarao Haldipurkar's house, who was former district Congress Committee President. We sent Bettegowda to stay at his place," said Anantrao.

"Now I am leaving. I will come back at night," said Rama Nayak. From outside he shouted, "Arre, you have thrown papers, newspaper pieces here. This will help the police to know some outsider is here. You Santu, come here. Pick up all these papers and burn them. There should not be a single piece of paper anywhere here. Anatraoji, tell this to all. In this deserted place if the police find paper they will suspect that some outside has come. Pick up each piece, and put it in the oven," Rama Nayak told the boys.

"Hello Rama Nayak, you had promised to bring Nilagiri (eucalyptus) oil for me. Yesterday I had severe headache. If we catch cold what are we to do? There is no other medicine here", Devayya told Rama Nayak in Kannada with Mangalorean accent.

"I shall bring it definitely tomorrow, or if possible tonight," Rama Nayak promised and set out.

After Rama Nayak left, Anantarao Chikodi asked Krishnaswamy: "Can you do stencil cutting?"

"Yes, stencil cutting and duplicating I know. In Bangalore Seva Dal camp they have taught us."

"Were you doing it at Bilgi? What other work were you doing there? These days they are not releasing the bulletin daily."

"Twice a week they were releasing bulletin from there. Now Pundlik Shenoy is doing it from another forest camp. I did not do the bulletin work there in Lambapur. I was doing fieldwork from Lambapur centre."

"Then you were with Premanand? It seems he is very sick. What happens to him is a matter of anxiety. The Visapur camp jail is like hell. Already Bairu Gowda from Uluvare village died in that jail. It is 10 days now."

"Premanand is sick? What happened to him?" Krishnaswamy was very anxious to know. "It is he who stopped the auctioning of confiscated cattle at Siddapur. What has happened to him?"

"Who can tell? Shamrao Shenvi of Ankola was there. His wife had gone to see him at Visapur jail. It seems Shamrao told his wife that Premanand is sick. From the day they brought him to the jail, he was having fever. What fever, nobody knows."

"Haa-Hoo," a loud signal was heard from the boys on watch.

"Arre, some danger awaits us. Now you remove your garments, spread them and sleep over it as if you are sick."

Again the sound "Haa-Hoo," was heard.

"Devayya, find out what is the matter?"

"Something from Hichkad side," he said after hearing a whistle. The cloths scattered over for drying inside were removed, folded and spread. Newspapers and two gunny bags were placed on the clothes and the bed was ready.

A boy came running and told them, that two plain clothes men and one in khaki dress were coming by boat. They were in the midstream. A woman from the neighbouring hut came running, put the duplicator in a big basket, covered it with leaves and a big plantain leaf. Over that she put cowdung, and she took the basket to the back of her hut. Devayya, dressed only in a *langoti*, hid all his dress, and taking a crowbar, started digging a half-finished pit some 20 feet away. Krishnaswamy was made to sleep on the bed, and asked to cover himself if the need be with a country rug. The other two closed the door and locked it from outside. They brought all fowls from the front house, and covered them with two baskets and placed them on the corridor of the house. They moved away towards the Joog shore. One of the boys, climbed up a tall tamarind tree, and hid himself at the top.

The visitors were policemen. They had heard that Koorve had given shelter to Congressmen. It took them quite some time to cross the river. The oarsman signalled their coming to the boys on the other bank and slowly rowed the boat. He took them to a point, far away from the residence of these people.

"Are there Congressmen here? Did Basgod Rama Nayak or Shetgeri Jogi Nayak come here?" the police asked the boy.

"Here at Koorve? Congressman? All Congressmen are in jail, right from Gandhi."

"Do they hold meetings here at nights? Do Jogi Nayak and Rama Nayak come here?"

"It appears Rama Nayak is arrested," said the boy.

"When is that?" the policeman asked with surprise.

"Many days ago."

"Who told you?"

"Hichkad people were talking."

This boy is a dullard, he does not know anything, the police thought. It took them half-an-hour to cross the river. One constable worried about his boots getting wet, removed them while alighting and a sharp fish shell cut his feet, and it started bleeding profusely. There was no piece of cloth to bandage it. He pressed it with his palm and sat on the bank, being unable to walk. Other two searched here and there and came near the huts.

In one of the huts, Krishnaswamy was sleeping. The door was locked from outside. In case the police broke the lock open, he was to tell them that he was sick. His wife had gone to fetch medicine, locking the house.

The constables were Konkana Marathas, who could not speak Kannada fluently. They came to Devayya who was engaged in digging and spoke to him in broken Kannada. Devayya behaved like a deaf and did not reply. They went to an inhabited hut. A woman held a basket and posed like going towards the sea. Having seen them, she stopped.

One of them questioned her: "Are Congress people here?"

"No one," she replied.

"Congress, Jai Congress people," he again asked her.

"Gandhi Congress," another man explained.

"They must be in Ankola," she said. The police entered her house searched it in and out. He went to the corridor of the locked house. Hearing their steps Krishanswamy inside was shivering. "The lady of the house has gone to Ankola to fetch medicine," the woman told the constable.

"Where is the key?" the constable asked her.

"Generally she leaves the key with me when she goes out. Today she has gone with her husband. So, there was no need to leave the key here," she said. "I will ask our other neighbour," she went to the other house and called loudly.

"Akku, Akku, you have Chandri's key with you?" There was no reply. She went into the house and came out. "There is nobody here," she said. "She must have gone to sea," Devayya gestured, extending only his hand. They asked him again. Devayya said 'yes' only by sign language.

The two constables went round the huts thrice. "Are you Congress?" the woman asked them.

"No, police, police," they said. She spread a mat in the yard of her house and made them sit. She asked Devayya to climb up the coconut palm and get them two tender coconuts and Devayya did it. After drinking coconut water and enjoying its kernel, the doubts they had in their mind faded away.

"Was Basgod Rama Nayak coming here?" one asked the woman in broken Kannada.

"Why should he come here? This garden belongs to Rayappa Sahukar of Ankola," she said.

"I see, I see, Rayappa Sahukar's," one of them repeated. The police left. They took as many fallen unripe mangoes and also plucked some from the trees. Half an hour after that, Anantrao came, opened the lock and 'released' Krishanswamy. All praised the women for their boldness and ready wit.

□□

# Naked Messenger

It was almost a week since Krishnaswamy had come to Ankola taluk. The Halakki Vokkals and the Nadavars were boldly resisting the atrocities committed by the government and the police. Women and children too participated in the movement. Houses and lands were being forfeited for non-payment of land revenue. There was only non-violent protest and resistance. The Nadavar men, known for their valour stayed calm, being bound to non-violence even when the police behaved high-handedly towards their women. Young boys from the villages resisted the police by irritating them. When the police caught hold of them and treated them inhumanly, they remained adamant. Their enthusiasm did not recede. Krishnaswamy heard many captivating stories of peoples' bold resistance.

Within seven days, after coming to Koorve, Krishnaswamy's foot got hurt by a fish shell, and he found it difficult to walk. Turmeric powder paste was applied and the wound was bandaged. He used to hold a stick while going to the call of nature. Though he went for fieldwork for a day or two later Mathand had to substitute him. Cutting stencil for the bulletin, rolling it, posting the bulletins by writing addresses, answering letters that reached them via Ankola, etc was his work. Suppose the police visited the place again, how should he escape from them? What kinds of situations will have to be faced? If the police come when he goes to answer the call of nature, how should he manage to escape as he could not run? In case he is arrested, the camp here will be known to the police, and the movement might suffer. This is how he was thinking all the while. No books were available to spend time. One day Rama Nayak brought him the bad news that Premanand Kalyanpur expired in Visapur jail.

He was with Premanand for only a few days. Premanand was polite, very good manager of things and well-versed in Hindi and English. He was well-read in economics, political science and religious matters. He always talked about free India. He was always dreaming and talking to people about his dreams. He had told them that he would settle down in Siddapur and teach the agriculturists better methods of agriculture, gardening, dairy farming and animal husbandry. He wanted Lushington Falls to be harnessed to produce power, help each village to develop home industries by using electricity, open co-operative societies and put end to many kinds of exploitation of the peasants. These were all his ideas. His death was not only a blow to the movement, but also to the country, Krishnaswamy thought. Hearing the news of his death all the four in the camp undertook fast on that day. Krishnaswamy could not sleep in the night. Next day he had fever. He started thinking that he too must become a martyr and join him.

When he had fever, he thought that he should not be there. In case the police come all of a sudden, all will be put to trouble. The strength of a chain is in its weakest link. A sick man like him will be a liability to the movement. Krishnaswamy felt that asking to shift him to some other place was cowardly. Then he thought that Premanand was calling him to join him. In case the police come, he should jump into the river and die, he thought. Those were the thoughts passing through his mind when he was in a delirium. He could do no work, not even prepare the bulletin. Other people in the camp took care of him with brotherly love. Nobody neglected him.

When Rama Nayak came in the evening, he thought of shifting him to Sagadgeri. "When Karmarkar came here in the beginning of the year, he was bitten by a *bukari* snake (A snake found in sand). His foot was swollen and he could not walk," said Rama Nayak. All the clothings of Krishnaswamy were packed. In the moonlit night, two persons joined their hands and made Krishnaswamy sit on their hands and took him to the river bank. The boat reached Sagadgeri in 40 minutes. Krishnaswamy was made to stay in the house of one Halakki Vokkal.

Rama Nayak told the household: "Look friend, the guest appears to be a Brahmin. Take care of him well. Nagappa Nayak will help you in all the matters."

Elderly Manu, her two sons, Sukru and Devu and Sukru's wife Tulasu were the family members. Manu took care of Krishnaswamy like her son. She brought some herb, pressed its leaves into a paste and applied it to the wound. She also gave him a herbal mixture for fever. In the meanwhile Rama Nayak sent a small packet of rice with a boy. The boy said that "Rama Nayak has said that the guest must be served *conji* of this."

"Arre, why all this. No no," Manu strongly protested.

"Rama Nayak has given this", the boy said.

"No, I don't want this. Are we incapable of serving *conji* to a guest? No, no. God will not like it. Return it to the person who gave it to you. Who gave this?"

"Nagappa Nayak gave this," the boy said.

"Tell Nagappa Nayak that he is in trouble having joined No Tax campaign. We do not want this. The person with merit (*punyatma*) who has come to our house is our guest. God has given us enough to take care of such guests. Take this back," Manu told the boy seriously.

Though they looked like very poor the richness of heart of his host made Krishnaswamy shed tears of joy!

Among the Halakki Vokkalu, only some families from Uluvare were land owners. They had all participated in the No-Tax Movement and had their own problems. The people of that caste in other places were landless labourers.

But they had all participated in Jungle Satyagraha (Forest Satyagraha), picketing of liquor shops etc and many had gone to jail. One Halakki Vokkal Satyagrahi had died in Visapur Jail. Rama Nayak had told about it to Krishnaswamy. Sukru and Devu were also active participants.

*Conji* was prepared and in the dull light of a small lamp, it was served to Krishnaswamy. He had no appetite. With great difficulty, he partook *conji*. But within half-an-hour after applying the paste to the wound, the pain slowly decreased. "Sir, do not worry. Sleep well. Tomorrow your fever will vanish", Manu said. Krishnaswamy felt as if his mother was treating him and was deeply touched by the innocent affection of the lady. The pain was almost vanishing he felt and he had sound sleep. Though the fever had subsided the next morning there was pain in the groin.

The old lady did not allow him to go out to answer the call of nature. She insisted on his easing himself in a broken pot and used a blanket as a screen for him. Krishnaswamy felt shy and uneasy. But, in the village he could not walk long distance to ease himself. Without showing any feeling of unease, the elderly lady took the broken pot out, cleaned it and placed it in a corner of the house. Even among these innocent villagers, a strange enthusiasm was created by the Gandhi wave and it was a strange phenomenon, felt Krishnaswamy. Otherwise how could these unknown people serve him? In what way were they related to him otherwise, he thought.

After he cleansed his teeth, and had mouth wash, they gave *hombesaru* drink. There was no fever and Krishnaswamy felt restless to simply lie down. There was nothing to read, and there were no books in the house of the illiterates. By about 10 in the morning. Nagappa Nayak came expressing his displeasure to Manu for sending back the rice. Then he smiled at Krishnaswamy.

"So long as our toiling arms are sturdy, and as long as we get labour outside, taking care of our guest is our duty. If I take the rice sent by you God will not like it", said Manu.

"How is your fever? And how is the pain?" Nagappa queried Krishnaswamy.

"This mother applied some paste in the night. Pain has come down. There is no fever at all. When I was in the camp, there were friends to talk. Some work or the other was going on. Here, lying down like this is boring. There is nothing to do."

"Pain will vanish in four to five days. That you are here is not known to anybody. Do not inform anybody, I have instructed Sukru and Devu. Ladies here also do not tell anybody. They are accustomed to give shelter to persons like you after the movement started. Our village has strong unity. Nobody leaks out news. Hear me, Manuamma, tell inquisitive people: It is Sukru's brother-in-law, who has come from Belambar and he fell sick soon after coming here. Have you followed me?" Nagappa Nayak asked Manu.

"This young man resembles our Tulsu's brother. The same age, the same height, is it not Tulsu?" Manu asked her daughter-in-law.

"Yes, our Pursu Anna is just like him," said Tulasu.

"Has he not gone to jail?" Nagappa Nayak asked her.

"Yes. He is still inside. He had performed Satyagraha. It is six-month term," Tulsu replied.

"In which jail is he?"

"I don't know. Belgaum or Idgi they were saying."

"Right, I understand. It is Hindalgi. It is near Belgaum. This girl's father's household is big. They are thirty. Three out of them have gone to jail. Some participated in Jungle Satyagraha, others in picketing liquor shops, etc. At Belambar, the Halakki Gaudas predominate," Nagappa Naik told Krishnaswamy.

"I was told Uluvare has greater population of Halakki Gaudas," Krishnaswamy said.

"Oh, at Uluvare they are the main landowners. Ramadas, Honnadasa, Sukru Gowda, Govinda Gowda, Devu Gowda and others live there. There are eight to ten landowners at Uluvare. They have all joined No-Tax Movement. They have suffered a lot. Their lands, their houses have been forfeited. Their family members have raised huts outside the village and are staying there. Akki Subbayya supplies rice to them as we do for other people who are thrown out of their houses. That is why he is called 'Akki (Rice) Subbayya.' Now their lands are to be auctioned. Nobody from this area bids for the land at the auction. We have to see the outcome. To arrest Ramdas, the police have surrounded the village and the hillocks ten times. Once the D.Y.S.P. brought a bus load of police. At that time, Ramdas was sick as you are now. He had stayed at Belse village in his brother-in-law's house. He could not walk. When the news came that the police with D.Y.S.P are coming, the villagers organised a harvest dance programme (Suggi Kunita). The European Saheb had great love for village dance, songs etc. He had not seen their dance. When he entered the village dancing was going on. 'Why have you arranged this,' he asked.

'We came to know that you are coming and you love our dance and song,' he was told.

"The Sabeb was highly surprised. 'Who told you that I am coming?' he asked, because it was all confidential official visit. 'Somebody told us, so we arranged this to welcome you,' an elderly man said. For half-an-hour, the colourful dance went on, and the Saheb enjoyed it. In the meanwhile Ramdas was taken away from where he was staying. The Saheb was happy over the entertainment arranged for him. 'These people here are not Congressmen, they appear to be pro-government. Otherwise, they would not have arranged a programme to welcome me,' the Saheb thought," said Nagappa Nayak.

"Who told him to do all this," Krishnaswamy asked.

"Nobody. But if Ramdas was arrested in our village, it was an insult to the village, they thought. But it would have taken much time to shift Ramdas. If the police party came, they would search every house. So, quickly the programme was planned. Till the time these artists could put on their dress, the players of drums and other instruments kept themselves busy on the spot where the dance was to be performed. By the time the police could reach there, the dance had begun, and they had time to shift Ramdas. Even then two policemen had come near the house where he had stayed. They had a clue, but five minutes earlier only Ramdas had escaped," Nagappa Nayak said.

"Had there not been forfeiture in Sagadgeri? I was told once they did."

"Thrice did they come for *japti*. Forty two landowners had taken pledge not to pay. Of these 24 houses were forfeited and receipt for the collection of revenue was passed. In our village, almost every peasant has his own land and also land taken on rent. They cultivate both the lands simultaneously. Lands on rent are owned by people in the town. Most of them would have paid their tax. In case they paid the tax, we had decided not to pay them rent. Later our leaders said that No-Tax and No-Rent programmes cannot be conducted simultaneously. Now No-Tax for freedom is important. Now our fight is against the British. We decided to pray to our landowners not to pay the Tax. Now only landowners in our village are yet to pay Tax. Forfeiture orders have been issued against them. At Kanagila they have pitched a police camp and they started forfeiture from the other bank of the river. The other day a funny thing happened. You don't know that?"

"What happened? As I had high temperature, I could not know anything."

"The Police had pitched a huge camp at Kanagila. On the other bank of the river the movement of our workers from one village to the other had become difficult. They arrested Palekar and Mahale there. Kanagila Hammanna Nayak hatched a plan. He is a fun-loving character. He organised the procession of Kalasha of Karidevaru. It was organised for the first time! Hundreds of women from the surrounding villages taking decorated pitchers on their head came in a procession with loud instrumental music. They came like possessed persons applying vermilion thickly to their face. The leader of the possessed persons shouted loudly, "In my path, who has created hurdles? The human sheep that has thwarted my movement will be destroyed together with his progeny.. I shall order my *ganas* (servants) *hoon, haan*," he shouted quaking his body deliriously. This was followed by ear-breaking loud instrumental music that reached the sky. The police in the tent came out, each placed a coconut as offering to the god and promised to remove the tent. They partially removed the tent and made way for the Kalasha procession."

"The police kept the promise?"

"They themselves removed the tent partially, as I told you. At night, our boys climbed the nearby tree tops, shook the branches violently. Created strange impish screaming sounds and threw small pebbles and sand on the tent and created terror in the minds of the 4 or 5 police camping in the tent. One even had fever. The police inside were terrified. Even before dawn they removed the camp and vanished."

The news caused profuse laughter in all including Krishnaswamy. The threat to the Koorve camp also vanished, he thought.

"Is this news not published in the bulletin?" Krishnaswamy asked.

"This has happened only yesterday morning. This news may appear today."

"Now they may have a camp on the other side of the river. You will be in their direct view."

"Let them come. What may come tomorrow, let it come now. Finally the issues have to be settled. You want tea or coffee? I shall get necessary powder for the same."

"No, no. I gave up taking coffee or tea a year ago when I was at Ranebennur. When in jail, I totally gave up the habit."

By then, a boy brought a bulletin, "O, Digambara, the bulletin has arrived."

"Just now Venkappa brought it." The Kanagila episode was reported in it. "God Karideva's fury on the police," was the heading. It was also stated that if God is furious at the government, the government will not survive for long." Having read the report, all had loud hearty laughter. There was also the instruction to celebrate Congress Day on May 1. The government's propaganda that Congress was totally defunct after jailing all the leaders had to be countered. So Madan Mohan Malavya had decided to hold Special Congress session in protest in Delhi on that day. On the same day processions and meetings were to be held at least in every taluk centre was the call. In addition, on May 4, Gandhi Day was to be celebrated.

"May 1$^{st}$ is day after tomorrow. Will I recover my health by then? Of course by May 4$^{th}$, I may be all right," Krishnaswamy said.

"What other news, Digambara?" Nagappa Nayak asked the boy.

"Why do you call him Digambara? Is it his real name?" Krishnaswamy queried.

"O, it is an interesting story. You yourself narrate it Digambara," said Nagappa Nayak. The boy was feeling shy.

"Three months back, he was carrying our mail, wrapped in a

*bhairasu* (small towel). 'Be careful, *tapal* should not fall into the hands of the police,' Karmarkarji had sternly warned him. He was to take it to Bankikodla to hand it over to Banduku Baburao. He used to mail it from Gokarna. Once police caught hold of this boy near Bankikodla. The police held him by his *udidara* (string round the waist that secured *langoti*). He, as is common, was only wearing a langoti. The *udidara* got cut and his *langoti* was carried away by wind. This Digambarappa ran away. The police pursued him. This boy swam across a stream, jumped over a compound and ran into a wet field. The constable fell into the stream. This boy ran almost a mile helter skelter. Then he took a plantain leaf, wrapped the letters in it and hid it in a sugarcane field, duly marked. He wrapped himself in the *bhairasu* in which letters had been kept and went to Baburao one hour late. Baburao got the bundle of letters with his help. He bought a ready made shirt and knicker for this Digambara, and sent him back by bus. From then on we call him Digambara."

"A historical incident," Krishnaswamy laughed loudly. "Look how teenagers too have presence of mind."

# Flag of Honour

On May 1st, there was a procession of 3000 people at Ankola. This was to celebrate the Congress Day. It included large number of women. It started from Gandhi Maidan (named so after Salt Satyagraha) after saluting the flag and it passed through all the streets of Ankola town. Majority of people in the procession were from the villages. They sang patriotic songs and raised slogans. About 20 police constables threatened that they would resort to lathicharge, and they hit some persons. But the procession continued. The police even threatened them that they will resort to firing. None bothered.

We will march ahead
Even if we have to die.
We are not afraid of canon
Gunpowder and bullets
We will tame the dictator with our love
We will win over him with our love.

This song was popular. The procession reached the Tahshildar's office and people squatted around it for an hour and dispersed silently after singing patriotic songs and shouting slogans. It was announced that on the $4^{th}$ of the month, Gandhi Day would be celebrated and all had to come again.

The next day evening, a police party with eight constables and a

Jamadar camped at Sagadgery. Is it time for his arrest, Krishnaswamy was worried. Though his fever had gone, the pain in the leg persisted and he could not freely walk. "As the police had come for the collection of revenue, you need not be afraid of arrest," Nagappa Nayak told him. By then Narayana Rao from Bangalore had arrived at Koorve and was supervising the camp work. Though there was a massive programme in Delhi on May 1st, Malaviya had not been arrested. In most of the places in the country Congress Day programmes were held, and reports also came in the newspapers. Government's propaganda that Congress is dead proved to be false by these programmes. The workers were now full of enthusiasm.

On the third of May, the forfeiture of the house of Govindaraya Nayak at Sagadgeri was announced by issuing notice. Govindaraya Nayak was arrested. Dozens of youth had assembled. Krishnaswamy covering himself with a country blanket and supporting himself with a stick went limping all the way and sat on a pipal tree platform, silently observing the developments. By hitting empty tins with coconut shells, the boys were creating nasty sound to irritate the police moving behind them. Police chased them and hit them by lathis. When they were hit, the boys shouted '*Mahatma Gandhi Ki Jai*'. Some boys were caught, they were made to sit in a corner, and two constables were put on sentry duty. The police hit the boys mercilessly but nobody protested.

The police ordered the residents of the forfeited house to vacate it. They were forced to quit despite physical resistance and were dragged out. Even women were treated similarly. They used foul words against women. One woman who had stretched herself on the chavadi was dragged out and hit with a lathi on her knee-joint. Krishnaswamy had heard of such acts, but now he was personally witnessing them for the first time. His blood boiled. But remembering Gandhi and the idea of non-violence helped him to retain his mental balance. He remembered the *shloka* '*Sthitaprajnasya Ka Bhasha*' from the Bhagavat Gita and chanted the whole of that portion mentally.

A man seated on the pipal platform said, "After all only ten constables have come to arrest these people. Why not tie them to a tree and burn them? They drag women and hit them as if they are animals. Nearly hundred men have assembled here and what are they doing?" Krishnaswamy did not open his mouth. His throat was getting choked. They dragged four women out of the house as if they were dead dogs. Finally two of the women came out on their own, one of them holding a baby. The other had wrapped herself in a country blanket.

"That is Govindaraya Nayak's daughter-in-law. She delivered a child just eight days ago," somebody on the pipal platform said.

"What evil days have come," somebody said. Two sons and two brothers of Govindaraya Nayak sat quietly in the courtyard of their house. "They are really the incarnations of non-violence," Krishanswamy said to himself. "Take these vessels with you," the police said and brought some earthen vessels from inside the house. One or two vessels were also broken in the process. One boy said that the British empire will also get shattered like the vessels. The Monkey Brigade was shouting slogans, and also singing songs loudly. It was quite a large group.

The police shifted their possessions to the house they had forfeited and camped in the house which was quite large. Govindaraya Nayak who had been arrested was asked to go into the house. He did not agree. He was sitting in the sun. Three constables in the evening took him to Ankola by foot after crossing the river. Some of the boys were beaten severely, and the boys ran away.

On that day, at Sagadgeri, no patriot took food, no oven was lit. There was peace, peace of the graveyard. The police who had occupied the house cooked food inside and had their supper. They plucked mangoes, raw and ripe in the compound and partook tender coconut water from coconuts plucked from the same compound.

In the night Nagappa Nayak came to see Krishnaswamy. It was rumoured that next morning the police would pull down the flag staff which the people had saluted that day. Krishnaswamy shed tears. That Manu and Tulasu had seen him shedding tears was not know to him. "If I were able to walk, I would have gone and embraced the flag staff. I would have told them that they should cut me first and then cut the staff next," said Krishnaswamy.

"What do you mean? Are there no men in the village? Even before seven o'clock, people will assemble here. We are prepared even to die," said Nagappa Nayak.

"Where is Govindaraya Nayak's daughter-in-law? I was told, she has delivered a baby just a week back."

"These messengers of Yama (*Yamadutas*) have thrown that lady out of her house. Don't they have a mother or wife or sister?" said Manu furiously.

"She has been sent on a cart to Hiregutti, her father's house. At Kanagila, a woman suffering from smallpox was thrown out of the house. Later she died. She had four children."

"Now who takes care of the young children?" Manu asked with compassion.

"Satyagraha is not an easy thing. People have to be ready to sacrifice everything including house, family and even one's life. Will the British simply leave? The Mari will leave only after all that has been sacrificed to her," said Sukru. An uneducated young man speaking these words sent Krishnaswamy into raptures. He had a sense of shivering in his intestine.

"Where are the members of Govindaraya Nayak's family? If possible I want to talk to them. But I can't walk."

"Today they are in our house. In a day or two the villagers will build a hut for them," said Nagappa Nayak.

"How strong will be such temporary hut? Will it sustain rain and wind? How about the children?" Krishnaswamy asked.

"Why do you ask such questions? Have they not anticipated all this? In this taluk 60 houses have been forfeited. This movement after all is Freedom Movement. Our leaders have drilled these ideas right from the days of Salt Satyagraha in 1930. People here have intense hatred in their blood towards the British. So much atrocities the British have committed here," said Nagappa Nayak.

Till now Krishnaswamy was working from behind the scene. But the fearful future of these people came before his eyes. He was rather frightened. What has happened at Kelaginamane? He heard of the arrest of Nagesh Hegde. Have they forfeited his house? Where are the ladies of the house? What may have happened in Paramayya's house? What Rukku might be doing? Rukku engaged his mind for a minute.

"What arrangement is made for their food and other necessities?", Krishnaswamy asked.

"From the relief fund we give them some rice and money. What we give is very insufficient. But people of the village do help them. If the houses of all are forfeited, God alone save them. Let us see how long will this continue. 'If Swatantryadevi is to arise from the sacrificial pit, our properties, houses, family and if necessary our life will have to be offered as sacrifice,' Diwakarji had once said. We do not know how much sacrifice she wants.. Rama had stayed in forests for 14 years. How long we have to live in forests, we do not know. Let us see….," said Nagappa Nayak.

All were silent for some time.

"Tomorrow's programme is fixed. Early in the morning, there will be flag salutation. Then *prabhatpheri*."

"Yes, in the morning we will salute the flag. What happens then, we have to see. People are prepared. Now I take leave of you," said Nagappa Nayak.

Much before Krishanswamy awoke the next morning, Manu and Tulasu had left home. Devu had been asked to take care of Krishnaswamy. "Where has your mother gone?," Krishnaswamy asked Devu. "She has gone for flag salutation," Devu replied. Having finished his ablutions and drinking *hombesaru*, Krishanswamy went to the pipal platform as he had done the previous day by wrapping himself in a blanket and holding a stick.

At a far off place from there, around the flag post about 50 to 60 people had assembled. Manu and Tulasu had woken up at 4.00 in the morning. Going from house to house calling women, they had gathered about 50 people. They sat round the flag post. The Police came with a machete to cut the flag-post. Women did not allow them to go near the post. They pushed the women around and went near the post. When they tried to cut the post, Manu and Tulasu embraced the post, preventing them from cutting it. No amount of threat by the police could deter them.

Tulasu was beaten by a cane till her skin peeled off. But Sukru was standing away silently. "Though he is known as a quarrelsome person, it is strange that he is quiet while his wife is being beaten," one person on the pipal platform said.

"He is afraid of the police," another person said.

"Don't say that. Is he afraid of the police? In that case he would not have stood here. Year before last, he had attacked Ugrani Devu."

"It is the influence of Gandhi's idea of non-violence. His wife and mother had brought our women. Today they came even before *belli* (Venus) rose in the sky. How old is the girl? She is from Belambar. People from her family have gone to jail," a third person seated there said.

"If I am well, I myself would embrace the flag staff and protect it," Krishnaswamy had said last night. That must have strongly urged the two ladies to take the initiative and leadership to protect the staff, Krishanswamy felt.

"What will be the final outcome of this movement? How long will people remain without paying the land tax? When all lands and houses are forfeited these people will have only to beg. In Ankola, all landowners have paid the revenue. In Siddapur and Sirsi also they have paid. If hundred people in one village do not pay, will it matter?" One of the men sitting on the platform asked. People heard him silently.

"Who told you that all the people in Siddapur have paid the tax?" one questioned lowering his voice.

"All that is government's propaganda."

"The caste men from Shimoga and Sagar and other places extend the Havik Brahmins of Siddapur hospitality if their houses and garden are forfeited. Brahmins can practice astrology, perform *poojas* in the temples and fill their belly. What can Nadavars do? If we lose our lands, are we to work as coolies?"

"We may do anything; who are you to question us? You have not joined the No-Tax Movement. You are living happily," was the reply.

"Those leaders from Dharwad and Mysore come here, stay hidden and advise you to undertake No-Tax Campaign. Have they resorted to pay No-Tax regarding their own lands? Has Karmarkar pledged that he will not pay the tax?"

"'We resort to No-Tax, you please lead us'," we requested Karmarkar. There is no land in his own name. Matanda from Kodagu has not paid land tax for the last three years. All those leaders came here to communicate Gandhiji's message. In Ankola taluk 600 landowners have signed the No-Tax pledge. Out of these only a dozen may resist till the end. Let Siddapur and Sirsi people pay, we shall not pay," another person said.

"All these are perverted ideas leading to total destruction – *vinasha kale vipareeta buddhi*," said the first one. Krishnaswamy was just hearing all this.

"If the country is being destroyed how can we survive? There are people who lick the boots of the British. Because of such dogs the country fell into the hands of the British. Grandchildren of Manthara or Jaichand are still there. To which place do you belong?" the protestor asked him loudly. The person did not respond. "He is a guest who has come to the house of Venkataramana Nayak, and he is from Madanageri, my dear," somebody said.

"You are from Madanageri? So long as you are in this village please keep your mouth shut. If Venkataramana Nayak's house and property are forfeited, he will not come to you even to taste the leftover *conji*. I have seen government agents like you. If you continue to talk like this, we will throw you out of our village by holding a procession."

On the platform, there was silence. But how many people were there to sow the seeds of poison all around, Krishnaswamy wondered!

The police by using lathis tried to disperse the mob from around the flag post area. The flag had been hoisted and the people there decided that they would not allow the flag post to be cut and flag lowered. Some 15-20 people were on guard. The police returned to their camp and by the evening everything was calm.

One sentry with a gun in hand was on watch at their camp. As it rained he took shelter in the verandah of the house. The Monkey Brigade from behind the house hoisted the tricolour with the help of a ladder. And they went to every house and told people not to co-operate with the police. The villagers were asked to fill their vessels with drinking and cooking water before daybreak and hide the ropes of their wells.

Early in the morning the police found the flag fluttering on their camp. They asked for a ladder from the neighbouring houses. Everybody refused to lend the ladder. The Ugrani threatened one or two women for refusing to lend the ladder. "If you arrest us on this pretext, please do," was their reply.

The Ugrani asked for ladder from the neighbouring Jug village. Message had gone there already and none was willing to lend. Even at Ulavare on the other side of the river, the reaction was the same. Finally at the time of a low tide a ladder was secured from the house of a Patel. While bringing it by boat, the oarsman made the boat's movement shaky, and the ladder fell into the river. The floating ladder could be caught only after it had moved near Jug village.

By then, at Sagadgeri the police went to the wells to collect water for their camp but, there was no rope. An old rope inside the house of Govinda Nayak was used by using an earthen pot. The rope snapped and the pot sunk in the well. In a village where they could not get a ladder, the police dared not ask for a rope. It was 10.30 in the morning. As he could not get tea, Jamadar was feeling uneasy. He remembered an incident that happened two years' ago in Singanamakki village. The people had boycotted the police at the time of No-Tax campaign. The police party had to face lot of difficulty. He ordered to shift the camp to Hichkad.

At noon in the hot sun, the Monkey Brigade shouted slogans and accompanied by the "empty tin-coconut shell" band, gave a farewell to the police party. But the flag was flying on Govindraya Nayak's forfeited house which was under lock. On a plank serving as a frontal screen, a boy wrote with charcoal a sign board 'Congress Office'. Police ignored the board. The flag staff was also safe.

When Krishnaswamy heard of these developments, he could not control his laughter. Tulasu, who was hurt by police caning had red marks on her skin. But she did not groan. She was treated with some

# Breaking the Salt Law

As efforts to collect revenue and forfeiture activities increased. To divert the attention of the police and administration, some major activities were planned. By consulting the workers of Kumta, it was planned to attack the Sanekatta Government Salt Depot for a second time after 1930. Salt was stocked at Sanekatta Depot. The excess salt which could not be stocked in the godowns there was thrown into the sea on 15 of May every year. Otherwise, the salt accumulated in the salt pans used to get washed off in the rainy season. It was planned that before the excess salt was thrown into the sea, people should take it and stock it for their household use.

Krishnaswamy, who had recovered from his wound went walking to Sanekatta. Rama Nayak had planned the attack. Villagers from Aggaragona, Jug, Sagadgeri, Uluvare, Moralle from one bank of the river, and those from the other bank of the river like Ankola, Hichkad, Kanagila, Shirur, Bole, Basagod, Shetgeri and many other places had assembled in hundreds. It was planned for May 12, and the assembly this time was far bigger than the one in 1930. People from the towns of Gokarna and Kumta had also joined. People had brought conch, jagate, drum, trumpet and other musical instruments.

There was nobody to guard the salt pans. People filled their bags, sacks, baskets and other containers with as much salt as they could. Slogans rent the sky. So did the sound of musical instruments. The police who came late arrested only five. But later they released three.

This programme added to the strength and momentum of the movement in the district.

Soon after, a secret meeting of the senior workers was held at Yana, a hilly track, which could be reached only by foot after a long walk. The wonderful rock formation at Yana took Krishnaswamy by surprise. After the meeting, Krishnaswamy was to return and work in Siddapur taluk only. So he came to Bilgi. He was there at the Bilgi camp for 3 to 4 days with Gulvadimam. The movement was very vigorous in Siddapur taluk. Field workers used to visit the camp at night everyday. They used to submit the report of the day's activity. Their number used to be between 10 and 20. The daring of these young men, coming in the dark of the night, walking in the jungle full of wild animals was unique. Patriotism alone was their guiding spirit. After collecting news from them, writing the day's bulletin and getting the bulletin stencilled and rolled was done by midnight.

Hot water boiled in tins was kept ready for them. After an oil bath, and hot *conji* they had sound sleep for a few hours. Taking the bulletin with them, they used to vanish before daybreak. All local and all-India news was included in the bulletin.

The high-handedness of the police and the officers, the bold acts of freedom fighters while facing the police, the ready wit of Satyagrahis, events of forfeiture, anecdotes of patriotism and other inspiring material was published in a foolscap sheet. Children and women took it to different villages.When the workers from the Bilgi camp took them to various places, those who could not read took the help of the readers and came to know all the details. The bulletins provided the workers in far off villages information to keep their morale high.

As the movement reached its climax, prizes were announced for the arrest of Dodmane Nagesh Hegde, Kariyappa Sangur, Gopal Hegde, Pundlik Shenoy and Gulvadimam in Siddapur taluk. Anybody providing help to arrest these men, or information for their arrest could get a prize of Rs.1000.

Gulvadimam, Pundlik Shenoy and Kariyappa Sangur were considered as 'dangerous' and there were orders to shoot them at sight. But none provided any clue to the police. The police were keen to know the whereabouts of Sardar Venkatarmiah, and the search was on in every possible way.

Rainy season set in. For the last two years, areca plantations had suffered due to plant diseases. Many peasants and coolies were starving. As streams and rivers were in spate food grains could not be transported from outside. Many peasants and the poor could not have cereals and they ate jackfruit, jackfruit seeds, sweet potato and other forest tubers to satiate their hunger. Grain stocks being confiscated from the No-Tax Payers, the participants in the movement were in dire distress. To help such indigent families, rice and a small amount of cash were being distributed by Congress. Akki Subbayya was in charge of it. Financial aid was sent from Bombay and from Bangalore via Shimoga. This was distributed from Centres at Koorve and Tadagalale. This assistance was hardly one-half of what the families really needed. This relief was given so that the Satyagrahis should not take to beggary and live with self respect. In both the taluks of Ankola and Siddapur, hundreds of families were reduced to this position. Yet nobody showed less enthusiasm towards the movement. It appeared that women showed more enthusiasm than men.

Five days after reaching Bilgi camp, Venkataramayya invited Krishnaswamy to meet him at Tadagalale. This place was a small hamlet in Sagar taluk and there were some 20 houses. From some of the houses of this hamlet and from other houses in neighbouring hamlets, Venkataramayya and his co-workers guided the movement. The police from Bombay Presidency could not come to the place straight as it was under a separate administration and this helped them to be in a safe place. There were occasions when the top authorities of the Canara District and those of Shimoga could work in coordination but by the time the police reached the place for any purpose, the persons would shift their activities to some other village. Even workers doing field work in Siddapur taluk stayed in Sagar taluk as Tadagalale was just 4 to 5 miles away from Siddapur taluk border.

After having met Venkatramayya, Krishnaswamy was deputed to Lambapur centre. He was addressed as 'Krishna Bhatta' as he was called earlier. He heard the news of Kelaginamane. There had been radical changes. Nagesh Hegde and his brothers were in jail though for short terms. Their house, lands and gardens had been forfeited. Women of the house with their children stayed in the houses of their relatives. Hegde's gardens had been secured by Chungadi Sambajja during the auction. Lands were secured by Latapati Vamanappa of Lambapura.

One night Krishnaswamy went to Paramayya's house at Kelaginamane. All the members of the family were very happy to see him. They felt that they had got back a valuable support that they had lost. Rukku was specially jubilant. On the way, a leech had bitten him and his leg was smeared with blood. The leech was removed by applying lime. He was made to take an oil bath. They heard about his activities since his departure. They also told him the story of Nagesh Hegde's family. Subraya and his wife stayed with Paramayya for some time. When their property was auctioned, the members left the place. The jewellery of the family might have been hidden somewhere nearby. Otherwise Subraya would not have stayed there for long, they felt. Dodmane Ramnath Hegde also had deposited their family jewellery with Nagesh Hegde. And one of the relations of Ramanath Hegde, Itagi Narayan Bhagwat also had once visited Nagesh Hegde and had a long discussion with him. 'These two families have caused me lot of headache,' was Nagesh Hegde's complaint. All these details were told to Krishnaswamy by Paramayya's family members.

"Whenever the police came, Ambakka used to go to a nearby jungle with a small covered basket. Once when she was going she fell down and was seriously wounded in the leg. After that, they must have put their jewellery in some vessel and buried it somewhere," Shivamma said.

"Now our land and garden is not forfeited. But if they had handed over the jewellery to us, things would have been difficult for us. These people do not cause inconvenience of any type to anybody. The Kite-Eye had only one aim—to destroy Nagesh Hegde's household. He tried to find out where the jewellery was hidden. In many places jewellery hidden underground was located. At Dasanahodlu, jewellery weighing 30 tolas, buried underground in the kitchen was unearthed.

Similarly at Tarkhand Hegde's house, all the jewellery of the women was confiscated. Even here, Sambajja with the help of the police, got the whole of Nagesh Hegde's house dug up. Not an inch of space was spared. The house looks like a cemetery. For full two days this excavation work continued," Paramayya explained.

"How long has Subraya been in jail now?" Krishnaswamy asked.

"Only four weeks. He is sentenced to three months. Ramakrishna Hegde has been in the jail for three months. What a tragedy. All four men of this house are in jail."

"I had been to Bilgi Pundlik Shenoy's house. Already seven men and one woman from the family are in jail," said Krishnaswamy.

"Who is that Shenoy? Are they the family of Madgaonkar Vaidyas?" Shivamma asked.

"Yes," said Krishnaswamy. "The same family. They are called Rajavaidyas. One man from this family, Pundalik Shenoy is underground. There is a shoot-at-sight order against him. The other members of the family vacated their huge house at Bilgi and are staying in a cottage near their lands. In India's North West Frontier Province, from every family 3 or 4 persons have gone to jail. Here you see dozens of such instances," Krishanswamy said.

"Is it true that Clee Saheb has resigned?" Paramayya asked.

"That was the rumour, When Puranik of Bilgi was arrested, widows conducted a procession in February. Then there was a rumour that Clee would resign. Commissioner Smart and Collector Clee it seems told the government that in Canara, people were in great distress due to failure of crops. If some concession was given to those peasants suffering from the failure of crops, the political agitation will also cool down. By suppressing the people, these problems cannot be solved. Their advice was not heeded by the government. They transferred Clee to Karachi. Now our own Indian, Keremath is posted as Collector. That is the rumour. The police are widely spreading news that the new Collector will get 800 strong locks, and he will lock all the houses of the 'No-Tax Payers' and seal them. Those men who have not paid tax will be buried to the level of their necks. The ladies in the house will be disrobed and beaten in front of their husbands. He will not free anybody till they pay land tax. He is no way inferior to General Dyer. That is the kind of propaganda the police carry on."

"O God, he will disrobe women and beat them? Oh Rama, Rama," Shivamma said beating her chest.

"Only when they do such things, they will lose their power. Did they not do it to Draupadi? From then the fall of the Kauravas started," said Paramayya.

"Don't you know that Kallala Kaveramma, and Gauramma Venkataramayya had been severely beaten by the police? Gauramma was the first woman to be arrested in Siddapur taluk. Mangoli, Sub-Inspector it seems, beat her mercilessly. 'I shall have your saree torn, I shall disrobe you' and many such foul things he told her. 'In case you do all that, I will commit suicide,' the lady told him in a determined voice. Pundlik Shenoy has written in the bulletin, that in case Keremath does any such thing, the ladies in the town must close their doors, bolt it from within, saying, 'O Fire God (Agni), this is food for you' (*swaha*) and set fire to their houses. Finally saving such women becomes government's responsibility. In case one or two such episodes occur, the British Parliament will be shaken. 'The moment we decided to join the movement, we had prepared ourselves to die. We are prepared to do as advised in the bulletin', some women have already said. Women from Pundlik Shenoy's house themselves were prepared for such an act," said Krishnaswamy.

"It is said that at Mavinagundi ladies have undertaken fast. Why this fast?" Shivamma asked.

"Some persons have purchased the forfeited items that were auctioned. To bring about a change of heart among them these ladies have resorted to fast in front of the houses of such buyers. This programme was planned by Venkataramayya. Somebody from Hecche in Sorab taluk bought such an auctioned buffalo. Those who have bought buffaloes belonging to the Satyagrahis must return the buffaloes was the message of the fasting Satyagraha. This was undertaken by Venkatramayya's wife and two other ladies. They fasted sitting in front of the purchaser's house. On the third day of the fast, the housewife of the house felt miserable and returned the buffalo. These ladies were honoured with an oil bath, and served a delicious meal. The buffalo was sent in a procession with *danapatra*. This has stopped people from Shimoga district bidding for the auctioned items of the Satyagrahis. After that there was a similar fasting at Shiralagi in our own taluk."

"Is it Gauramma who undertook the fast there?"

"No. It was Duggamma of Hanajibail, Shiralagi Parvatamma and Bhagirathamma who undertook fast. They were arrested and later released in the night. Next day they resumed their fast at the same place. After 22 days, the buyer finally surrendered," said Krishnaswamy.

"Fasting for 22 days!" Shivamma exclaimed.

"Yes, full 22 days. Similarly at Akkunji, Gauramma undertook fast. When she was arrested by the police, other women continued the fast. They included Dodmane Mahadevi and others. Madgaonkar Seethabai, Pundlik Shenoy's sister in law, who had delivered a baby three days before, also joined the fasting women. At present such Satyagraha by ladies is continuing at Mavinagundi and Tigane in Sirsi taluk. Today it is Bhuvaneshwaramma's 22nd day of fasting. Lakshmamma's, 9th day. Lakshmama is fasting for the fourth time."

"She must be a great woman," said Shivamma.

"You know the other details about her. Police came to arrest. Lakshmamma's husband Timmanna Bhatta, He said, 'Today is Shivaratri. I will perform *pooja*. You please take *phalahara* (items taken in lieu of regular meal).' So saying he served the police with jackfruit, bananas, milk etc. 'After my pooja, you take me,' he told them. In the case of many Satyagrahis who were served warrants by the police who came walking from far off places, the person to be arrested asked them to take their food in his house. He too finished his meal and he surrendered to the police and accompanied them to the far off lock-ups. Such instances are quite numerous in our taluk. The police had known such instances. Timmanna Bhatta told his son to keep ringing the small *pooja* bell in the *pooja* room, and escaped from the back door into the forest. After the *pooja* of their own stomach was over, the police called Timmama Bhatta loudly saying 'Finish your *pooja* early.' The bell was still ringing. But on search Timmanna Bhatta was not there. The police angrily fired a gun shot. Timmanna Bhatta heard the gun shot and escaped over the border into Sagar taluk. The police told Lakshmamma that her husband was dead. They left empty handed, abusing her. Timmanna Bhatta did not return.

"When Venkataramayya sent for her, she met him at Tadagalale. He consoled her by saying that her husband was very much alive. 'Are you prepared to undertake fast?,' he asked Lakshmamma. Both this lady and her daughter-in-law Kaveramma agreed. Together with Gauramma, these women too were made to don saffron saris, wear garlands, and decorate the forehead with large vermilion mark. Playing instrumental music, they were taken in a procession to the site of fasting. Timmanna Bhatta who had gone somewhere, saw the procession and his wife, and was so much overtaken by ecstasy, he bowed down before both his wife and daughter-in-law and addressed his wife as "Mahataayi" (Great Mother). He applied vermilion to her forehead. Lakshmamma was overwhelmed. Her joy knew no bounds as her husband had blessed her. Now, this is the fourth time she has undertaken fast."

"Had you been to Mavinagundi to see them fasting? How are the fasting women? Have they not become very weak?" Shivamma asked.

"I was thinking that I must go. But on the 4th June there is Gandhi Day programme. This is the fifth month after Gandhiji's arrest. We have arranged a group prayer in front of the Lambapur temple. I have to prepare for that. After that I shall go. I was told that the Havaldar at Mavinagundi is causing them lot of trouble."

"Who is that Havaldar?"

"He is the person from Mavinagundi who has taken an auctioned item. Mostly Patels, constables, government servants and Ugranis are the persons who have bought the auctioned items of the Satyagrahis at very cheap rates. Mavingundi is a small place with 20 houses. There are only some young volunteers to help the fasting persons. If any one of us goes, they will immediately arrest him. Only in the darkness of night we can visit the women and talk to them. Mhala Bhatta and Gopala Hegde from Siddapur do visit the place. These ladies have squatted on the corridor of the Thana (Chauki) of the Havaldar in the night. At times he does not permit them to sit on the corridor even during the night. Once he pulled their saree and used abusive words. He engaged a bully to hit them with a piece of wood. The people in the village boycotted the bully and took him to task severely. The Havaldar threatened the people. 'We boycott you also. Return the buffalo you have bought,' they said. 'The buffalo is not with me,' he said. He had handed over the buffalo for safe custody to some villager nearby. Identifying that villager Gunjgod Mahadevamma and another lady went to the villager's house, undertook fast urging him to return the buffalo. The villager got frightened seeing the shouting of the Monkey Brigade. He returned the buffalo to the Havaldar. Now the Havaldar has hidden the buffalo in another labourer's house.... We have to watch and see what happens. The correspondent of the Madras English paper *Hindu* who came for reporting has also been arrested."

"Now there are only two women. Mavinagundi is a small place. Even in the night if these women sit like that, what will happen?", Shivamma asked with anxiety.

"It is like Rajput women prepared to perform *jowhar.* They have worn saffron saree. 'We are even prepared to die' they say; even if it rains, they do not leave the place. To take care of them, volunteers from a distance keep observing them. If there is any trouble, they shout and people assemble. Nobody is with them because persons are arrested if they try to join them."

"But this is really pathetic," said Shivamma.

"See Shivamma, at Sagadgeri in Ankola taluk, I was staying in the house of a Halakki Vonkkal family. Last month on Gandhi Day, the police came to remove the flag staff. The daughter-in-law of the house where I stayed, Tulasu, a fifteen year old girl, of the same age of your Rukmini, went and embraced the flag staff. Police hit her with lathi and cane, and blood started oozing. The police could not remove the staff. When women were applying oil to the girl's wounds, she was saying, 'Sukru Anna, my brother, will be overwhelmed with joy by this news.' In fact her brother is in jail at Hindalga."

When Krishnaswamy mentioned her name, Rukku's face turned red. Should I too not get an opportunity for such an adventure? she thought.

"In Ankola women have been adventurous. As you undertake fast here, they break the seals of forfeited houses. Nearly sixty houses have been forfeited in the taluk. Some houses have become police camps. In a village called Vasre some ten houses have been forfeited. Heroic Manudevi from Hichkad village entered a sealed house by breaking the seal open. The police dragged her out by holding her hair and sealed the house. Again she entered the house. She was severely beaten, dragged out like a dead body. They threw her into a gutter in front of the house. She lost consciousness. People thought that she was dead. The police ran away. People admitted her to Ankola hospital. She recovered after 4 to 5 days. Again she came to Vasre and entered the same house by breaking the seal open again. Now she is arrested. Boys, like Abhimanyu, enter the movement with all valour. At Hichkad, a boy called Narayana Nayak was beaten till he became unconscious. This boy is of the same age as of your Shankara. He is active even now. At Koorve, he is the volunteer at our camp. The stories in Mahabharata or events of Rajput history are repeating before our eyes. And this is non-violent warfare. The Nadavars are a martial race. But when their women are manhandled by the police, their hair is pulled and sarees are dragged these men stand looking like incarnations of non-violence. In a village with a population of 300 or 400 persons, some four or five constables indulge in such atrocities. It is strange but true. It is a miracle that illiterate villagers stand quietly without losing their temper, while such inhuman acts are perpetrated. Not one or two, but hundreds of people witness their atrocities without retaliation. In all the villages it is the same story. The movement was started just six months ago. Those Nadavar women, who never leave their house except to work in their fields, now are willing to court arrest and go to jail in places like Hindalga, Pune and Visapur where the language spoken is not known to them. It is really inspiring."

□□

# Tiger!

"Leave it, leave the photo, leave it, you whore, we shall cut you into two," the police shouted pulling the plaits of the girl. Rukku did not speak but sat on the ground, holding the photo frame tightly. She bent forward to tighten her grip on the photo-frame. Two constables tried to loosen her grip by pulling her arms. They did not succeed. They hit her arms with a lathi. The Monkey Brigade loudly shouted slogans. One constable held her ankles and another tried to pull her shoulders. Two other constables were trying to disperse the boys by swinging their lathis.

"O Dusshasana, who pulled Draupadi's sari," now became the slogan of the boys. Rukku fell flat on her back, and the photo frame of Gandhiji she was holding fell on the ground. Its glass cover was broken to pieces. In the meanwhile 2 to 3 ladies, unmindful of lathi-wielding police came near Rukku and surrounded her. The broken glass pierced Rukku's arm and it started bleeding. Within 2 to 3 minutes more women came on seeing the blood. The constables became nervous. Catching hold of two boys, they moved away. Remaining 20 to 30 boys ran behind the police saying that they also must be apprehended.

Rukku was treated by bandaging the wound; she was given water to drink. Later a tender coconut water was offered to her. She refused to take it. The glass sheet of the photo was partially broken. They decorated the broken frame with flowers and one held it on her thigh and they started singing patriotic songs and Gandhiji's pet song 'Vaishnava Janato....' Some men also came. Earlier they had stood as onlookers and later joined in singing. This all happened during the Gandhi Day celebration in front of the Lambapur temple on 4th June. As the police did not come again, Krishnaswamy came to the spot. Seeing him, Rukku's joy knew no bounds. In the company of another lady, he took her with him, congratulating and praising her for her valour. Other persons continued the *dharna* and singing.

Rukku was taken to the house of a friend who was sympathetic to the movement called Nagesh Shastri. They gave her *sherbat*. As her sari was torn, the lady of the house gave her another saree and asked her to change.

The news reached Kelaginamane. Shivamma and Parvatamma came almost running to Lambapur. Shivamma was glad to see Krishnaswamy there. "You are here, Krishanbhava, that is our solace. Where is the wound?" Shivamma asked.

A Satyagrahi called Ramachandra Bhagavat, who had participated in the Satyagraha had been sentenced to six months jail term. He was from the hamlet Sungolimane. He was in Visapur jail, which was a very unhygienic place, where he fell sick. He had loose motion. He could not bear the fatigue. He wrote an apology, got released and returned to his place. It was more than three weeks. Knowing the news of disturbance at Lambapur, he came to Lambapur. Hearing that Rukku was at Nagesh Shastri's house, he reached the place. Seeing Rukku wounded, he felt highly disturbed.

"It was a mistake that I apologised. I shall join the movement again," he told Krishnaswamy with folded hands. "I am prepared to go to jail again. I shall definitely go," he swore.

Shivamma, Paravatamma and Ramachandra Bhagavat came to the spot where dharna was held till dusk.

That evening Krishnaswamy went to Tadgalale and met Venkataramayya. A worker called Deshpande from Dharwad had come to meet Venkatramayya. He was working at a place called Huvinamane in Siddapur taluk. As he was working in the jungle area, he suffered from scabies. One day he applied oil to the body and took a hot bath. There was a burning sensation over the whole body. He wanted to apply some more oil. But none of the Satyagrahi families in the neighbouring villages could spare him a few drops of oil, because they themselves didn't have it. Oil and butter milk had become luxuries to them as everything had been forfeited, including milch cattle. They used to take their meals (*conji*) early, hide their vessels out of fear of police visit, and they would cook food only in the night.

During day time, they almost fasted, eating fruits or nuts, which included jackfruit, *mogekai* (cucumber), dry-fried jackfruit nuts, and forest berries, etc. There was no use of oil at all.

"Without milk, buttermilk, curds, butter or ghee, how can their children grow? Will it not be a weak generation?" Deshpande questioned Venkatramayya with great anguish. It was a genuinely serious question. "Suppose we ask them to send the children to our custody, will they send?" Venkatramayya asked.

"What do you mean by 'your custody'?"

"We shall take all these children and make arrangements to take care of them in a secure place. There are instances where in some houses both husband and wife have gone to jail and their children have become almost orphans. There are four or five such families. With such children and those whom you can send, we shall arrange a Children's Home and take care of them," said Venkataramayya.

"The idea is good. But how many parents are prepared to part with their children?"

"In such cases, ask the parents of such children to come. They will be the staff to take care of the home."

This idea took shape when a Balakashram was started in Shimoga. A similar shelter home was opened at Karwar also. Children of many Satyagrahis who were in jail were given shelter in these places. Such children were also admitted to schools in those towns. Well-meaning and national-minded people in those towns managed to run those shelter homes for which separate buildings had been engaged in both the places. Shimoga had about 60 children. Seva Dal men like Vasudeva Rao, Matanda, M.N.Jois from Mysore and his wife Subbamma took care of the Shimoga Ashram. The last two had offered Satyagraha in

Canara, gone to jail, and got released after their term was over. Some people who were keen to offer Satyagraha and go to jail left their children in the shelter and courted arrest.

"Dodmane Nagesh Hegde's house in Siddapur town was auctioned and Uppadike Samayya bought it," Kannalli Shivarama Hegde from Siddapur told Venkatramayya the same day.

"Till now not many houses could be auctioned. This is a morale breaking development. Bring that Samayya here, we shall tackle him," said Venkatramayya.

On the same day Krishnaswamy went to Mavingundi as instructed by Venkatramayya. Bhuvaneshwaramma's fast had reached 30 days. He reached the place in the night. He ate food at Siddapur and took a volunteer from there. It was raining and Krishnaswamy was bitten by leeches.

In the dead of night, there was the sound of barking dogs and no human was to be seen. In such a situation, the women were fasting. Krishnaswamy was very much agitated. As they went near the Thana, two boys came running.

"Who is that?" one of the boys asked.

"Is it Ira?" person coming from Siddapur asked.

"Yes, I am Ira. Is it Narna?"

"Yes. This person has come from Tadagalale," he introduced Krishnaswamy to the boys.

Pointing his finger towards the Thana, Krishnaswamy asked, "How are they?"

"They have just gone to sleep. Both of them are sick. Bhuvaneshwaramma was complaining of stomach ache. Lakshmamma is coughing and vomiting. There are two more women with them. Let us go a little away from here. They may get up." They went some 20-25 steps away from that place.

It was an old large choultry. Though it was a tiled structure, it was all dripping inside. Three boys and one youth were sleeping there. In one corner they had lit a fire by piling firewood. Things were visible because of the fire.

"How have they permitted you to stay here? Is the Hawalder

keeping quiet?", asked Krishnaswamy. Taking a small tin box containing lime from his pocket he tried to remove two leaches that had stuck to his leg.

"He threw us out twice from here. But we came back. For the last four days he has not come. He has gone for *japti* work, they say. Two constables are there. Today the Havaldar's wife and children went to Siddapur. They are under boycott. They could not stay here as nobody supplied them milk," one of the boys said. Krishnaswamy and Narna's clothes had been completely drenched. They removed them and squeezed out the water as they talked.

One of them named Pandu told the other, "Krishna go to Rama Hegde's house, and bring a mat, two *panches* and a *kambli*. Tell them people have come from Tadagalale.... Or, would you go there? How about your supper?" he asked Krishnaswamy.

"We have taken food at Siddapur. Don't wake up anyone now, at this odd hour," Krishnaswamy said.

"At least you can go there to sleep, your dress is wet. Here the roof is leaking and it is also very cold."

"Do not worry. I shall stay with you. I have to talk to you," Krishnawamy said.

"Then you Krishna, go to Rama Hegde, and bring the items as I have told you, go quick," Pandu said and sent Krishna.

"Bhuvaneshwari Amma is very weak. What will happen tomorrow nobody can say," Pandu said with tears in his eyes.

"Why, is she so sick?"

"Today it is the $30^{th}$ day of the fast. Jamadar was very arrogant initially. Now he has mellowed down. It looks like he was telling the Patel here five days ago, 'Enough with their buffalo and enough with their Satyagraha. But if I return the buffalo what will the government say? What am I to do if action is taken against me?' After that he has not come back."

"Is that so? To that extent Satyagraha has won. There is a change of heart," said Krishnaswamy.

With the clothes brought by Krishna, Krishnaswamy and Narna changed their dress. Spreading the straw carpet both Krishnaswamy and Narna stretched themselves. A broken laterite stone was used as a pillow.

"Tomorrow morning Dodmane Mahadevi Tayi and two other women are coming before seven. You wake me up at five o'clock," said Krishnaswamy.

He had started on foot from Tadagalale at five in the morning and had reached Lambapur. Meeting and instructing the workers there, he had taken food and started to Siddapur again by foot in the sun. At Siddapur, he had his food, and despite the rain, he had come to Mavinagundi. His legs, waist, back—every part of the body was aching.

When he got up early in the morning, ladies from Siddapur had come though it was raining. Bhuvaneshwaramma's fast had reached the 31$^{st}$ day. Her condition was precarious. The news that she could die had made people from many surrounding villages to assemble. By about 8.00 in the morning a coolie came dragging a buffalo and said, "Jamadar has told that you must take your buffalo," so saying he left the buffalo there and wanted to walk away.

"The buffalo was left in his house. He is Hanjakki Tippa," one of the volunteers said.

"Where is Jamadar Saab?" a lady questioned him. But he did not reply. Krishnaswamy asked the volunteers to stop him and get a letter with his signature or thumb impression with two witnesses saying that the Jamadar had asked him to hand over the buffalo.

That the buffalo had been returned became big news and a huge crowd gathered. Sloganeering rent the sky. By then women from Ram Hegde's house brought boiled milk and made Bhuvaneshwaramma and Kallal Kaveramma to partake a few spoons of the milk. The fast ended! The Monkey Brigade prepared a thick garland of wild flowers, put it round the neck of the buffalo and paraded it like an *ashwameda* horse. Somebody brought drums and other instruments.

Krishnaswamy made arrangements to return the buffalo to its original owner. The police took the fasting women under their custody. Locals gave the women tender coconut water to drink. The police took them to Siddapur by bus and produced them before the magistrate who sentenced Bhuvaneshwaramma and Kaveramma till the court ended. They were later admitted to hospital. Krishnaswamy returned to Siddapur by foot, had his food at Durgappa's house and started to reach the Bilgi camp.

He had to go through a forest. It was soon dark and he could not find the path to the camp. It was dark and raining. His footwear got buried deep in the mud. For almost an hour he wandered in the jungle. A thorn pierced his foot. It made a deep wound. He removed the thorn and it was bleeding. But he could not see anything. He could not walk anymore. Road to freedom is full of thorns and stones, he told to himself. In a jungle full of wild animals and snakes, it was not safe to move in the dark. He sat on the thick trunk of a fallen tree. It sheltered him from rain too. Let me move only when the day breaks, he thought. He was feeling hungry. He remembered plantains given to him by Durgappa. He ate them. Leeches were kissing his legs and in the darkness he could not see them. Some wild fly bit his leg and it caused burning pain. He was seated there for almost an hour. Then he saw two people moving at a distance with a burning torch in hand. Are they policemen? It is better to be caught by the police than being eaten by wild animals, he thought.

"Oy, please stop," he shouted. They stopped with utter surprise. Without caring for thorny prickly bushes and creepers, he ran to them. Then he realised that they were workers from Bilgi.

"What were you doing here Sir?" one of them asked.

"I missed my way to the camp. There was no light too. I was just waiting to see if someone would come," Krishnaswamy said.

These two persons were regular visitors to the camp. He joined them. He told them about the victory at Mavinagundi. The news had already reached Bilgi. They were happy to hear the first hand details.

They reached the camp. Removing the leaches and thorns, Krishnaswamy took hot water oil bath, had his food and went to bed. But the pain caused by forest fly's bite irritated him. Bulletin was ready covering the Mavinagundi victory. But he could not sleep. Then he saw that somebody had lit a campfire behind the camp. Two of them sitting there were dozing. He too joined them in dozing in front of the fire. He had a short nap.

After sometime, he heard somebody breathing loudly. Krishnawamy awoke. He smelt some foul odour. He opened his eyes. In front of him, on the other side of the fire, a huge tiger was squatting, warming itself by the fire! As its body was wet due to rain, it was emanating foul smell. Even in the heat of the fire, Krishanswamy started shivering. It appeared to him that the tiger was staring at him. Suppose he moved or tried to run away or shout, how would it react? He held his breath and sat motionlessly. The small logs put in the fire had their ends burnt and the fire was getting dull. He dared not push the logs further. But it appeared that in the next few minutes the fire would get extinguished. The fire must be brightened. But what would be the tiger's reaction? After sometime the tiger turned its face. What was the next move? It stood up on its fours. It shook its body violently and created a fluttering sound. One of the other two opened his eyes. Krishnaswamy closed his mouth so that he may not shout. The jungle king slowly went away!

The experience had lasted 20 minutes but Krishnaswamy felt 15 to 20 years had passed by! His other friend had urinated out of fear. To the believers of non-violence, the tiger was also non-violent, felt Krishnaswamy.

Next day Krishnaswamy went to Siddapur and bought a new pair of footwear. When he talked of the need for a torch, a freedom fighter gave him his own torch and he also bought a pair of new batteries to recharge the torch.

□□

# Brave Bommakka

"The police took all members of Hasalarakeri of Bijjala to a forest and threatened them severely," Krishnaswamy was told by Paramayya when he went to Kelaginamane.

"What for?"

"The police have a doubt that Nagesh Hegde's family members have buried their family jewellery in the premises of their confiscated house. That is why not only the house, but also their kitchen garden, front yard etc., were dug up. They got nothing. The police thought that those who live on the *maradi* (hillock) at Bijjala might be knowing. A woman called Devi and her old husband were harassed. It appears the police fired a gun shot towards the sky to threaten them."

"What happened finally?"

"Shoot me, not God," it seems Devi said.

"What does it mean?"

"Firing at the sky is shooting at God is her concept. Poor innocent people are being harassed. They are all very, poor. They work here in the gardens and farms and earn their livelihood. As most of the gardeners have gone to jail, they have no earnings and most of the coolies are spending hungry days."

"How do the police know that Nagesh Hegde might have buried the family jewellery?"

"The Kite-Eye might have told them. Who knows?"

"God alone has to save. How is Rukmini? How is the wound?"

Krishnaswamy enquired.

"Now I am all right. There is a little pain," said Rukku coming out boldly from the house. She showed him the wound by unfolding the bandage. On her round rosy tender arm, the wound looked like a polished ruby fixed in an ornament.

"The flesh inside is visible. In a week, the whole thing may get healed.... Will you join Satyagraha in some other place? Now at Tigane women are fasting," Krishnaswamy joked.

"Oh, I am ready," she replied.

"After the Satyagraha in which she participated, now she feels that she can go anywhere," Shivamma said and served *happala* and *kashaya* to Krishnaswamy. Krishnaswamy left early for Lambapur.

*Japti* action was in full swing. Though some forfeited fields and houses were auctioned, in the majority of cases, properties could not be auctioned, as there were no bidders. Hundreds of acres of forfeited lands could not be auctioned, and they were entered as fallow lands in government records. The crops in the forfeited lands were harvested by Satyagrahis going in large numbers, as the police could not check them. A large number of Satyagrahis who had been released from jail after completing their term formed "Raid Parties." Nearly hundred people in 2 to 3 groups were undertaking this venture. Those who had bought the property in auction were feeling frustrated and helpless. Those who had bought properties in a far-off place could not get coolies to harvest the standing crop. The coolies also sympathised with those who had lost their properties. There was a strong patriotic propaganda among the coolies also. Many labourers collected forest products, fish shells, pounded rice and undertook other sundry jobs and managed to live. But in Siddapur town some locals did buy such properties with great enthusiasm. This very much irritated and caused worry among the Congress workers. Uppadike Samayya Hegde, a loyalist, bought the farm house of Dodmane Nagesh Hegde which he had at Siddapur town. This he could secure by paying a few hundred rupees though it was worth thousands. As the people in the town were unhappy about it, he had secured two police guards to move around in a majestic style. He had gun license and he used to carry the gun on his back while moving out. "You must bring him once to Tadagalale," Venkatramayya had instructed Kannalli Shivarama Hegde, a leading worker from a place near Siddapur.

When Krishnaswamy went to Tadagalale, Shivarama Hegde and another worker expressed their sorrow about the difficulties they faced.

"We brought him physically lifting him for a distance of three miles. But he was resisting us by violent movement of his legs and hands. Finally we left him at Mugadur and took out the papers he had in his coat pocket. It was very difficult to control the brute," said Kannalli.

"I had not told you to bring him here by physical force. You somehow manage to bring him here was my suggestion. When you tried to physically force him, now he is sure to file a police complaint against you," Venkatramayya said.

"What shall we do now?" asked Kannalli and Bayalalli.

"We don't want these papers of his. You go to Byadgi and send these by registered post, addressed to the Tahshildar of Siddapur. We will think over this matter later," said Venkatramayya.

Kannalli gave Krishnaswamy other details. They laid an ambush to catch hold of Uppadike Samayya. But he was always moving with his gun and police guards. He had been working against the movement and had helped the police to arrest many underground workers. Two days earlier, as usual, he had come to a hotel at Siddapur. He asked the guards to wait at the entrance of the hotel and ordered his favourite dishes. Bayalalli knew the hotel owner and had asked him to add some purgative in the dish to be served. After finishing his tiffin, chewing betel leaves he started boasting how he is a favourite of the government. But the purgative did its job. He wanted to go near the Puttayyana Kere (tank) to ease himself. He called the guards to join him. 'You did not invite us while loading yourself. Why do you call us while unloading yourself? We won't come,' was their reply. Samayya literally ran towards the tank. Left his gun and coat. He washed himself at the tank. Bayallali and Kannalli Shivarama Hegde who were hiding near the tank on the hill, caught hold of him with the help of his upper garment on the shoulder. They lifted him up physically and took him to the road to Tadagalale. But they could not carry him for long because of the violent movements of his hands and legs. He was not shouting out of a sense of shame. They dropped him there and escaped. Hearing the news, Krishnaswamy did not know whether to laugh or weep!

Soon after, Dodmane Nagesh Hegde, Shiralagi Subraya Bhatta, Kannalli Shivarama Hegde, Bayalalli and other Congress workers numbering 40 persons were charged with attempt to murder him. Uppadike Samayya Hegde lodged a complaint with the police. Warrants were issued to arrest Kannalli and Bayalalli and others. After this incident nobody came forward to bid for the forfeited property. Rumour was Red Shirts from Peshawar had come to catch hold of Uppadike Samayya Hegde.

Those who had purchased the items or properties that were auctioned faced the music of women fasting in front of their houses. Nearly 40 women had participated in such programmes. There were fasting *dharnas* at Bilgi and Tigane.

*Japti* and arrests continued in September. When imprisoned Gandhiji undertook fast over the issue of the practice of untouchability in Pune. There were programmes all over the district to propagate eradication of untouchability. At Sirsi, local Congress leader Keshavain took initiative in taking the Harjans to Sirsi Marikamba temple. Krishnaswamy had participated in the programme. On return to Lambapur, he arranged such a programme at the local Ganapathi temple. Harijans from Kelaginamane, Danamavu, Bijjala, Sungolimane and many other surrounding places came in procession, singing *Ramdhun* and were taken into the temple. Devi from Bijjala whom the police had threatened, was also invited. Many Brahmin men and women participated in this mass temple entry programme together with people of other castes. Though some conservative persons opposed the idea, when they came to know that Gandhiji had undertaken fast over the issue, there was almost unanimity over the issue. Rukku had gone to Bijjala and brought Devi and her other castemen to the programme. Men like Patel Sambajja and others severely criticised the programme.

After some days, Kelaginamane Ramakrishna Hegde was

released. He decided that all members of his family must jointly undertake Satyagraha. The wives of the three brothers who had stayed in their parental house, four of his sisters, one sister's daughter, his mother and Shivamma and Rukku, all decided to break the seal of their house at Kelaginamane which had been forfeited. Accordingly they broke the seal of their house and entered the house. As the police had been informed earlier, almost a dozen people were arrested, but Rukku was released as she was a minor. Three men and eight women, four of them widows, were sent to jail. Subraya was already in jail. This unique example of a large family including highly conservative widows with shaven heads (who normally do not take even water from other places) going to jail, was an inspiring episode, and a record in Siddapur taluk.

Next day Krishnaswamy went to Kelaginamane. Rukku was the only person living in her own house with her siblings. She was feeling highly perturbed. Parvati Hegde was her only companion in the neighbouring house. There were chances of her house also being forfeited and her going to jail.

Finally Krishnaswamy took Rukku, her siblings Shankara and Saraswati to Karwar and left them at the Balakashram there. He had to cross many ferries and travel by bus to take them to Karwar. Rukku was day-dreaming all along.

Paramayya and Kelaginamane Ramakrishna Hegde joined the 'Raid Party' to harvest crops in forfeited fields and courted arrest. Kelaginamane Subraya Hegde was released from jail. The very next day he came to Lambapur. Krishnaswamy welcomed him with a hug. He went out and returned to Lambapur. He was found highly depressed on his return.

"Why Subraya, you look very dull? Is it because your family members are in jail?"

"No Krishanbhava, we lost everything of ours."

"When everything is lost, a Satyagrahi has to be happy. In Bardoli in Gujarat, the peasants whose property had been confiscated had celebrated it by a lamp festival (*dipotsava*) to express their pleasure, it was reported. When we attain independence, your sacrifice which was maximum, will be celebrated."

"Not that, not only ours but the belongings of others are also lost...."

"If other's items are gone, why worry yourself. When you are not worried about your losses, why bother about other's losses?"

"No, not that. Our honour itself is lost," Subraya started weeping.

Krishnaswamy could not understand the strange situation. "Why shed tears? How is your honour lost?"

"Krishnabhava, jewellery and valuables of our family, together with the valuables of two other families were put in caskets and buried on a small hillock near our land. Now all the three caskets have vanished?"

"Aan!", said Krishnaswamy with great surprise. For sometime both were silent.

"Yes, Paramayya was telling me. Police also knew it. How they came to know nobody knows. They dug up inside your house, backyard etc. Last month, they huddled all members of the Hasalarakeri, threatened them severely, even by gunshots to get any clue about it," Krishnaswamy said.

"If we lose our jewellery, we don't mind. Some serious allegations may be made by the other two families that I have swindled them. They may say that our family is of cheats. Our family's fair name will be tarnished."

How to come out of this crisis, worried Krishnaswamy. He used to go everywhere with Subraya as his companion. Subraya was almost mentally deranged. Taking care of him became an extra responsibility for Krishnaswamy.

As Narayanrao was arrested in Ankola, Krishnaswamy was asked to go to Ankola. He left Subraya at Bilgi, and went to Kanagila in Ankola taluk. Many houses of Naḍavars had been forfeited and the movement had reached its climax. But people had not lost their enthusiasm. During the last week of November, the Governor of Bombay was to visit Karwar. Basagod Rama Nayak desired that he must be greeted with a black flag. Many Nadavar youth and others travelled to reach Karwar. But they were arrested and detained. There was strict police vigilance. But Kanagila Bommakka volunteered to do the job. In a bus belonging to Martappa of Honavar, accompanied with a volunteer, she travelled a day in advance to Karwar. Krishnaswamy also joined her. They stayed at a school near the Balakashrama that evening. Krishanswamy was happy to see Rukku there. Her mother was in Thana jail together with other women from Kelginamane. Her father was in Visapur camp jail. She knew that from a letter received from Gangadhar Shenoy who had founded the Karwar Balakashram. She told all that to Krishnaswamy.

Next day at the function attended by the Governor, Bommakka shouted loudly from among the crowd. "Governor go back", "Governor go back", in Kannada and waved a black cloth. The police and the public were highly surprised. When the police were trying to apprehend her, handbills telling "Governor go back" came flying like locusts. Where from they came, nobody could make out. A volunteer named Shirur who had accompanied Bommakka had climbed the top of a nearby tree and had thrown the handbills. A favourable wind brought the pamphlets to the venue of the meeting. The police, instead of apprehending Bommakka became busy jumping, hopping and running around to collect the pamphlets flying in hundreds. Bommakka escaped in the confused situation.

Even after the strong movement had been suppressed in Gujarat, it was still going on in Canara district. The Governor was surprised, the bulletin reported. There was appreciation of Bommakka's daring in the bulletin. Bommakka became a household name.

□□

# Krishnaswamy Attains Martyrdom

Spacious wetlands forfeited at Uluvare were purchased in auction by Bahadur Khan, a retired military officer. To guard the crop in those fields, a small batch of police had been deployed. The houses of Halakki Vokkals who were owners of these fields were demolished, and finally they had taken shelter in a hilly forest area. The wide fields of Uluvare where sugarcane was cultivated by Ramdas and others was ripe for harvesting. Satyagrahis earnestly wished that the sugarcane crop should not fall into the hands of Bahadur Khan. Nearly 300 youth marched and harvested the standing crop, singing heroic patriotic songs. Seven or eight police who were in a far off *chauki*, came and beat the harvesters mercilessly with lathis. The Satyagrahis did not bother about the severe beating and continued the cutting of crops. They bundled the cane and took them away despite opposition from the police. Many were wounded due to police blows and some were bleeding. Some even lost consciousness. But they neither retaliated nor indulged in violence. The sugarcane was harvested by the evening.

In the evening Bahadur Khan reached the place with two bus loads of police. By then there was not a single cane in the field nor were there any Satyagrahis. Innocent people who were moving round on their routine work were caught hold of, taken to the *chauki* and severely beaten and persecuted. To know the names and leaders who had taken away the cane, the police made all kinds of efforts. The Satyagrahis had come from many villages, and none knew their names. Some women were slapped with footwear and one or two lost their teeth. This kind of persecution went on for many days and many innocent people suffered.

The police had come to Sagadgeri and had arrested Tulasu who was severely beaten. Krishnaswamy came to know of this. Krishnaswamy remembered that she had compared him to her Pursu Anna. He was highly upset. He thought that he should go to the police *chauki* and tell the police sub-inspector that innocent people and women should not be persecuted. He came till the ferry. But later he thought that if he behaved rashly he might also be arrested and his part of the duty pertaining to the movement will suffer and do harm to the movement. From nearly 20 workers who had come from outside the district during the previous week, Channa Basappa, Deshpande, Kamalamma Chandur, Chinnappa and Devayya were arrested. Krishnaswamy feared that he may also be arrested.

He was standing on the river bank and was just thinking that he should go back and continue the work. "Please wait sir," somebody called him from behind. The person laid his hands on his shoulder. "You are from Mysore state, are you?" he asked. He was a policeman in plainclothes, Krishnaswamy could make out. He did not reply "Please come, our Saheb wants to see you," said the policeman. Another policemen joined him. Krishnaswamy thought of escaping by running away. But that would be an act of cowardice, against the concept of Satyagraha, he thought. Near the ferry the policemen took him to a *jungal* (bigger boat), and crossing the river, the three walked to the Ankola Police Station.

The officer there interrogated him.

"Are you Krishna Bhatta from Sagar?"

"No, I am Krishnaswamy from Bangalore."

"You are a Congressman?"

"Yes."

"One Krishna Bhatta from Sagar is said to be here at Kanagila as per reports. You know him?" Krishnaswamy laughed.

"You don't know? From Siddapur he came to Kanagila last month," the officer asked.

"I am the person. They called me Krishna Bhatta."

"O, this is impersonation."

"No. They called me so, that is all, I have not told anybody that my name is Krishna Bhatta".

"I see. Your father's name?"

"Chenne Gowda."

"Oh, you are not a Brahmin?"

"No."

"Then, how Haviks hosted you in their houses?"

"Why not? Congress knows no caste. Christian, Muslim, Lingayat, Vokkaliga, Kuruba, Harijan – Congressmen of all castes are welcome in all the houses of Haviks or Gowda Saraswats or Nadavars. They stay there, take food and do the work assigned to them."

"You did not introduce yourself as a Brahmin?"

"No, never."

"Our reports speak of you as a Brahmin."

"All people might have thought that way. I have never said that I am a Brahmin. One's caste has no place in the Congress movement. I had been advised to put on a sacred thread. But I never did it."

"What is your caste then?"

"I am a Gangadikar Vokkaliga."

The sub-inspector was confused by the caste name.

"We are agriculturists, Vokkaligas. Gangadikars are a section among the Vokkaligas," Krishnaswamy explained.

"Your age?"

"Twenty-two."

"Address?"

"Cubbon Road, Bangalore."

In the night Krishnaswamy was lodged in Ankola lock-up. Mahale and Pai, two Satyagrahis from Ankola were also there. For the whole of the night Krishnaswamy had nausea and back pain.

Next day he was taken to the court at Ankola. Krishnaswamy did not accept the allegations levelled against him. His only reply was he had nothing to say to all the questions asked by the Magistrate and the Prosecutor. He was sentenced to two years' rigorous imprisonment on charge of sedition. Pai and Mahale were sentenced to one year imprisonment on some other charge.

On the same day all the three were shifted to Karwar Jail. In the barrack to which he was admitted, there were Mahabala Hegde of Kelaginamane, Sagadgeri Govindaraya Nayak and his two sons. The Jail was full of prisoners. When Krishnaswamy told the news of sugarcane harvest from Bahadur Khan's fields, the disappointment caused to Bahadur Khan became an enjoyable big news. For the whole day Krishnaswamy had neck and back pain and was having nausea.

After having gone round like a potter's wheel Krishnaswamy had some relief in jail. But he was not feeling physically comfortable. He must be suffering from some ailment, he felt. Once he vomited. In the afternoon when he returned from his labour of breaking stone into pebbles, Mahabala Hegde put his hand on his shoulders.

"Arre, you have fever?" Hegde said.

"Yes, yes, I have fever," Krishnaswamy said. "From yesterday I am feeling highly uneasy. Is there high fever? In the morning I took bath too."

Before evening the news of his illness spread in the jail. The Jail Superintendent was a doctor. In the evening he examined him and gave some medicines and tablets. He vomited once or twice.

Next morning Krishnaswamy thought that he was feeling better. In the morning he performed his ablution. There was severe back pain. The Doctor came and examined him. Temperature was higher than that was the previous day. He vomited twice. Some other medicine was administered. That he had smallpox was soon realised by the doctor. He was removed to a segregation ward. They had diagnosed his fever as something else. The medicine he was administered affected him adversely. Except for one or two nurses there was nobody near him. Krishnaswamy was in a delirium. He dreamt of having gone to Kelaginamane with Premanand, where Rukku gave them milk to drink.

Finally he heard Rukku shouting the slogan, "*Bharat Mata Ki Jai*". He also said "*Bharat Mata Ki Jai*," loudly. The hands he had kept on his chest slipped to the sides.

The nurse shouted: "Mary, Mary, quick the patient is struggling."

Mary came, felt his pulse and said: "O God! Call the doctor, I think it is an end."

She stood up and invoked God by making a sign of Cross.

Next morning the news spread in the jail. All jail mates fasted on that day. In the evening Gangadhar Shenoy also heard the news. Shankar at Balakashram ran into the kitchen where Rukku was spinning Charkha.

"Akka, Akka, Krishnabhava died in jail, they say."

"Who? Who?" Rukku asked.

"The same Krishnabhava of Sagar. Some days back he was taken to Karwar jail. He died of smallpox. He was buried." Rukku was shocked.

Rukmini became silent.

Next morning, her body was found hanging from the roof of the kitchen.

□□

# The Long and Winding Road

Some died due to the high-handed acts of the government. Many lost their houses and properties. Till the month of May 1933, Mass Civil Disobedience continued, and on May 9$^{th}$ the Mass Movement was temporarily suspended according to the instructions of the then All-India acting Congress President Lokanayaka Aney. Till then in Canara district, more than 100 Khathedars in Sirsi taluk and more then 200 in Yellapur taluk were counted to have participated in the No-Tax campaign. A total of 420 landowners in Siddapur and nearly 400 in Ankola did not pay the land tax till the end. In these two taluks there had been nearly 1000 instances of forfeiture. Nearly 1000 persons from the district were jailed. This included 100 women and 20 children. Among the women there were highly conservative widows from the Havik and Gauda Saraswat Brahmin communities. Totally illiterate Nadava women were also there. These women were lodged in jails in far off places like Thana, Hindalagi, Ratnagiri, Yaravada and Visapur jails. They partook food which they never had eaten under unbearable circumstances. Halakki Vokkal families of Uluvare having lost their lands and houses had to live without a shade worth the name. Thirty-three families in Surve village lost all their lands. In Vasarakudrige, Kanagila, Hichkada and other villages, many landowners lost their lands.

In Siddapur taluk 104 families had lost their lands and elsewhere

76 other families had become paupers. About twenty families shifted their residence to Sagar taluk and started their life afresh. There were some instances of this kind in Yellapur and Sirsi taluks also.

□

"Odeya, my Master," Devi called loudly. Subraya did not hear.

"Master, I am Hasalara Devi," Devi ran to him and bowed before him. "My master, all your caskets are with me. Come to my hut, and I'll give them to you."

The face of Subraya which was dull and lifeless blossomed like a flower. She signalled him to follow her. "The caskets are with you?" he asked. She nodded. They walked to Bijjala near Devi's secluded hut.

"All the three caskets I have preserved on the attic of my hut. Will you take them?"

When Subraya heard her telling about three caskets, he believed her.

"How did you get them?" he asked.

Devi explained.

It was rainy season. They had no food to eat. As she was hungry in the morning she went to Nagesh Hegde's backyard where on an elevated ground there was a banyan tree. It had many tree-caladium plants (*marakesu*) on it. She wanted to collect tubers from the plants and climbed the short tree. The rays of the rising sun made her see something shining at the base of the tree. Rain water had washed away the top soil. She got down and scratched the place. She could see the casket and identify it as one belonging to the house of Nagesh Hegde as they had paid her money from it. She pulled it out. Then she saw two more behind it. She could understand what it was all about. She turned towards Sun God and prayed that evil thoughts should not enter her mind. She replaced them and covered the hole with a thick layer of mud and put a few twigs of shrubs to hide the spot. At night she brought a torn gunny bag, wrapped the caskets in it, and took them home and hid them in her attic.

Police had caught hold of Devi and threatened her, to know whether she knew about Subraya Hegde's hidden jewels. In the meanwhile ten days ago her sick husband had died.

"Shiva died? Oh God," Subraya beat his forehead with his palm. "Here our house has gone to the custody of Patel Sambajja. Garden and lands have been auctioned. We all now stay at Dombe near Sagar," said Subraya.

"Lands?" Devi asked.

"We are cultivating lands belonging to somebody else."

"O God, what a pity, what bad fate," Devi wept. "Now it is already night. Take these things as early as possible."

Devi opened the gunny bag cover and all the caskets with their locks were intact. "Take it away immediately Master, before somebody sees them".

"Devi, you are Goddess Devi's incarnation," Subraya said and opened one of the casket's lock with the key he had attached to his sacred thread. He took two gold bangles from one of the casket and offered it to Devi.

"O my Odeya, please do not tempt me with unearned money. We are people who earn our livelihood by the labour of our hands. If I take these, God will not like it, God will not like it. No," she flatly refused, and said, "You please leave the place immediately."

"Yes Devi, I will leave. I shall come again…. You come to Dombe, Devi. Meet all our people."

□

In Siddapur Magistrate court, hearing of the cases was going on. The defendant was Bayalalli Ganesh Hegde. He had been accused of an attempted murder. He had no advocate to defend him. Gulvadimam had sent him to Bangalore before his arrest and had him trained by a noted nationalist advocate Sampige Venkatapatayya. He surrendered to the police. He prayed to defend himself in the court and was permitted to do so. He started interrogating the complainant.

"Mr.Uppadike Samayya Hegde, at the Puttayyana Kere at

Siddapur, myself and Shivarama Hegde have tried to kill you is your charge. Is it true?"

"Yes" said Uppadike.

"You were frightened after seeing us?"

"Yes, I was very much frightened".

"Why? Did we come to push you into the tank?"

"No," said Uppadike after some hesitation.

"By pushing you into the tank it was easy to kill you."

"What do you mean?"

"Say 'yes' or 'no'"

"You did not push me."

"Could we not have pushed you?"

"What do you want to say?" said Uppadike.

"He is asking you whether it was not possible for them to push you into the tank. Answer properly," the Magistrate said.

"Yes, you could have pushed me and killed me," said Uppadike.

"Did we push you into the tank?"

"No."

"Was there anybody near the tank except we three?"

"No"

"We could have killed you by drowning you in the tank and escaped, is it not?"

"I can't say," said Uppadike.

"Please answer my question. Was it not easy to kill you then?"

"Yes."

"Did we kill you?"

"What does it mean?" said Uppadike.

"Did you die that day, please reply," said Bayalalli.

"No, you did not kill me, I did not die."

"Did we not tell you to accompany us and come with us?"

"After binding me physically and hitting me."

"No. We did not hit you. We asked you to come with us to Sagar. Is it not? You refused to oblige us. We tried to take you to Sagar, and you reluctantly came till Mugadur. You were unwilling, you shouted. Then we left you at Mugadur. Is it not?"

Uppadike did not reply.

"We left you at Mugadur without killing you. Is it not?"

"Yes," said Uppadike.

"Mr.Uppadike, you and your wife are not on good terms. Is it true?"

"In what way is it connected with this?"

"Such questions should not be asked," the prosecution advocate said.

"Your honour, I am to be hanged if I am found guilty. Give the dying man a chance," Bayalalli pleaded.

"Let him ask the question," the Magistrate said.

"Mr.Uppadike, your wife does not stay with you because of the strained relations between you. She stays at her father's place at Keladi in Sagar taluk."

"Yes."

"Your father-in-law has often written letters to you requesting you to come to his place. Is it true?"

"Yes."

"You didn't go. Is it true?"

"Yes."

"Your Honour, my examination is over," Bayalalli said. After other formalities were over, Bayalalli argued his own defence. "Uppadike's father-in-law who happened to be my friend had repeatedly pleaded with me to bring his son-in-law to Keladi. It was a fact that I and Kannalli Shivarama Hegde had tried to escort Uppadike to Sagar, as he was hesitating. But at Mugadur, all of a sudden he changed his mind and ran away. He has purchased in an auction the house and garden of Congress leader Dodmane Nagesh Hegde. Out of hatred towards Congressmen, he had petitioned against 40 Congress workers and of them some are in jail for more than four months. They were not with the accused at all. The complaint is far from true. If we intended to kill him, only we two could have done it. Myself and Shivarama Hegde also tried to persuade him to come to Sagar. For such a job, 40 persons are not necessary. Except we two the other persons are not connected with this episode. Many of them were in jail at that time and still are. We two never intended to kill him as alleged. All that is false." The Magistrate refused to commit the case to the Session Court and dismissed it. The elderly Magistrate was to retire soon. He did not wish to act recklessly.

Then they produced Devi.

"Why have you brought her?", the Magistrate questioned.

"This woman got a pot full of jewellery in the forest. She has not surrendered it to government. Now she has given it to Kelaginamane Subraya Hegde. She has committed a crime under the Treasure-Trove Act," the Police Jamadar said.

"Where is the gold pot?" the Magistrate asked.

"We do not know. May be it is with Kelaginamane Subraya Hegde."

"Is it here? Where is Panchaname report? Where is the *mudde malu* (item in question)?"

"Patel Samba Hegde will depose on the subject."

"Has he seen the pot taken by this woman?"

"Samba Hegde will depose."

"Have you arrested the person who is in possession of the pot?"

"No."

"The item involved is not there. The person accused of possessing it is also not there. The Panchanama is also not there. How can you file a suit? Look here, Amma. Did you find a pot of jewellery?"

"No, I did not find a gold pot," Devi replied.

"Why have they arrested you and brought you here?"

"I do not know, Odeya."

"From where have you come?"

"I came walking from Bijjala."

"Did they hit you on the way?"

"No, Odeya. They shot at God in the sky. 'Instead of shooting God, you shoot me,' I pleaded with them."

The Magistrate was highly upset.

"Nonsense. You have no other job to do? You have brought the poor woman in the sun on foot from such a distance. I can't accept such cases. Release her," the Magistrate ordered.

Devi was proved innocent.

□

When Gandhiji came to Siddapur in 1934, Devi was brought in a procession to Siddapur accompanied by instrumental music. When her story of honesty and her selfless help to a Satyagrahi family was narrated, Gandhiji was overwhelmed. Gandhiji touched Devi's shoulder and said: "Because of the presence of such *punyatmas* (meritorious souls) the world is sustained."

People who had lost their lands in 1932-33 had to undergo grave sufferings. To give an account of their fasting and suffering, space here is insufficient. They were treading the long thorny and stony path to freedom.

In 1937 Congress won elections to the Bombay Presidency Assembly and formed the government. The government passed an order to return lands, gardens and houses forfeited by the government in the No-Tax movement to its original owners. Those lands of the Satyagrahis which had been declared as fallow were also returned to their original owners. But lands that had been auctioned were secured back by the Ministers themselves who came from Bombay. Chief Minister B.G.Kher returned the lands of Uluvare Ramadas Nayak which had been taken by Bahadur Khan. The lands were returned to Ramdas with the minister symbolically performing the ploughing act!

The property of Dodmane Nagesh Hegde at Siddapur town had been purchased by Uppadike Samayya Hegde. Home Minister Morarji Desai personally came to restore the property to Dodmane Nagesh Hegde. Uppadike came to meet Morarji. He came with his gun dangling at his back. Morarji was furious. He ordered the confiscation of his gun and cancellation of the gun licence. All these acts were matters of solace to the Satyagrahis who had suffered humiliation for long.

Still the path for freedom was long! It was a thorny path!

□□